'This is, without question, the most beautifully written, sensitive, balanced account of grieving that I have ever read. This book is going to be an absolute "must read".'

Patrick Casement, psychoanalyst and award-winning author of *On Learning from the Patient* and *Learning from Our Mistakes*

'When she was young, Tara suffered two terribly cruel losses in quick succession. The compounded grief could have left her emotionally wiped out for life, but instead she learned from it in a most profound and moving way. She is now one of the bravest people I know, a woman of great competence working as a firefighter. She is an emotional and a physical warrior. She knows vulnerability well, but has learned how to live beyond loss, to make a meaningful life. Her story will stay with you and inspire you for ever.'

Dr Margo Orum, psychologist and author

'Tara's inspiring story takes therapy and moves it into real life. Her resilience comes from tenacity, intelligence and openness to new experiences. She persisted with study, work and relationships, using her courage and adaptiveness to create a life worthy of her and the people she loves.'

Tony Merritt, clinical psychologist

'This is the honest and at times raw telling of the story of a strong but vulnerable firefighter as she struggles with, and is transformed by, the legacy of grief associated with the childhood loss of loved ones. Those on a similar journey will find guidance, inspiration and reassurance in this open, he

psychologist

'I loved this book. So many times it expresses fears and doubts that we all have, in a succinct and yet profound manner. Tara's gift is to involve readers so completely in her journey that they, as I did, see the parallels in their own lives. I found it truly inspiring.'

Clinton Batty, psychologist

Standing on my Brother's Shoulders

MAKING PEACE WITH GRIEF AND SUICIDE

TARA J LAL

WATKINS

Sharing Wisdom Since
1893

This edition published in the UK and USA 2015 by
Watkins, an imprint of Watkins Media Limited
19 Cecil Court
London WC2N 4EZ

enquiries@watkinspublishing.co.uk

Design and typography copyright © Watkins Media Limited 2015

Text copyright © Tara J Lal 2015

Tara J Lal has asserted her right under the Copyright, Designs
and Patents Act 1988 to be identified as the author of this work.

9 8 7 6 5 4 3 2 1

Designed and typeset by JCS Publishing Services Ltd,
www.jcs-publishing.co.uk

Printed and bound in Europe

A CIP record for this book is available from the British Library

ISBN: 978-1-78028-902-1

www.watkinspublishing.com

CONTENTS

Everything finds its place, just as the colour and the beauty do, so does the pain.

Adam Lal

ACKNOWLEDGMENTS

It would be an understatement to say that when I started writing I didn't really know what I was doing. It was simply an organic, often painful torrent of words from within. I rarely read books and the extent of my previous writing experience didn't stretch beyond putting together scientific essays about cell membrane transport or the like, and that was over two decades ago.

Without question, this book would not exist were it not for the many wonderful people who offered incredible help, love and guidance, professionally and personally. In some cases their assistance was essential to the process of writing; others were simply there for me. Every interaction helped me sculpt the story of my brother's and my life into the book you are now holding.

So, from the bottom of my heart, thank you to the following people for allowing my dream to come to fruition.

To the team at Watkins, for believing in the book and its power to help others. Most especially to Fiona Robertson, for her incredible expertise and guidance in putting it all together to make something that in my eyes is both beautiful and valuable.

To Margo Orum, without whom I would never have put pen to paper, for it was she who made me believe that I could write. She ever so generously read my first garbled draft, encouraged me to continue and outlined some of the basic laws of writing. This book would not have been written without her!

To Wanda Whitely, my fabulous manuscript doctor, for her incredible patience and skill in turning my 80,000-plus words of disjointed gush into a story that flowed and actually made sense. Most of all, for believing in my work and for going way above and beyond the call of duty time and time again.

To Justine Taylor, for her fabulous editing and incredible attention to detail as she gently questioned why I had randomly changed tense mid-paragraph and corrected my seemingly infinite grammatical errors.

To Laetitia Rutherford, for her complete faith in me as an unknown author and for tirelessly approaching publishers on my behalf when I felt lost in a world I knew nothing about.

To Susan Burton, for her wisdom and skill as a therapist in ever so gently taking me back over the pain of the past while I wrote this book, with the perfect balance of empathy, care and professionalism. It was Sue who helped me make peace with the past.

To Steve Williams, for his creative genius in designing a concept for my book cover which turned my ideas into images that said a thousand words.

To Mum, for those golden moments of affection I still treasure, for enduring so much to give Jo, Adam and me the lives we've had, for instilling in me the values I still hold so dear and for allowing me to truly know the value of a hug.

To Dad, for always trying to be the best dad he could be, for allowing me to publish what is personal and painful to him and for giving me the freedom to follow my heart.

To my aunt, Margaret Coleman, for saving me; for holding my head above water when the grief threatened to swallow me up; for allowing me to live and express my pain. I am forever indebted.

To the entire Kaub family: most especially to Helga for being my Australian mother, for picking up the pieces every time I fell apart and inviting me into her family unconditionally. To her daughter Samantha Heron, for being another sister to me, for being the most generous caring person I know, for being my biggest fan and for relentlessly supporting and loving me.

To Jessica Hepburn and Beth Beamer, my childhood school friends, for their timeless friendship, for all the giggles, past and present, and for the many wonderful, insightful discussions we shared about the book.

To my Australian friends, Heather Shepherd, Kirsten McCaffery, Abigail Hatherly, Salvatore DiMuccio and Carly Reeves, for living the ups and downs with me, for sharing the tears and the joy. I could not have travelled this path without their constant support and love.

To my dear friend Stacey Siegert, for all the world analysis we shared and for helping me heal more than she will ever know. May you rest in peace.

To the Sydenhams, the Bruggens and the Stewarts for offering to adopt the three of us and for caring for and supporting us through our darkest days.

To Dan McAlister, for being the most loyal, caring friend to Adam and for being with me while I screamed.

To D Platoon, Darlinghurst Fire Station, 2007–2011, for giving me a sense of belonging, for always making me laugh, for the best-ever cook-ups, the hugs and never letting me get away with anything!

To Elouera and North Bondi Surf Lifesaving Club for giving me my passion back, for the incredible teams we created and for introducing me to the wonderful community of surf lifesaving.

Lastly, to my sister Jo, for coming up with the perfect title for my book, for her love and generosity which I never appreciated, for her honesty in telling me like it was, even when I didn't want to hear it, for making me an aunt to her two beautiful children, Marli and Asa, and most of all for supporting me in telling our story in the way that I remember it.

For Adam
May your beautiful soul live on through the pain and
eloquence in your writing. May it light a candle of insight
for others to live with greater connection, greater meaning
and greater purpose.

FOREWORD

Adam Lal was a school friend who committed suicide aged nineteen. It was a death I found hard, and never stopped finding hard. Five, ten, fifteen, twenty years after it happened, memories of Adam still had the capacity to jolt or glaze me. I'd feel my voice threaten to catch if I spoke about him.

I found this surprising in some respects. We were friends, but not best friends. It made me wonder if I mythologized him. And he was so *easy* to mythologize: he had such a glow, and died so young. Then I would remember something particular he said or did, or look at a photograph, and think: no. The qualities I ascribe to Adam, he had.

I was also trapped by specific conversations in which Adam had tried to talk to me about the nature of his unhappiness. I would picture him, sat cross-legged, halting as he spoke, often looking away. The exchanges haunted me – along with the knowledge that although I had understood the words he was saying, I had missed the meaning and the depths.

Then, a few months ago, I got an email from Dan, who features in the book you hold now. He told me that Tara Lal had written a memoir that substantially addressed her brother's suicide, as well as many other things besides. He arranged for me to get the manuscript. And almost as soon as I started to read, it was as if a light began to shine.

In part, the light was pure information. There were things in Adam's family history that I hadn't known, such as the nature of his father's illness, and the crushing weight this placed on Ad. I also found it incredibly uplifting to catch glimpses of Adam in Tara's portrait of herself, and to realize that something I thought had gone had not entirely gone.

But more than either of these things, the light came simply from Tara's writing. The thoughtful honesty in her words, and the compassion, and the truth, and the strength.

By the time I finished the book, Tara had laid to rest something fundamental about how I feel about my long-dead school friend. I can still miss him, and think about him, and the strength of that feeling is undiminished. But there's a clarity about it now. And the clarity is not just about Adam, and the circumstances of his death. It's much broader and more universal: about the way death reverberates through the lives of the bereaved, and the means by which we can process this.

In these terms, Tara's book will be important to any reader. All of us have either faced loss, or will face loss. Her insight helps.

Alex Garland

PROLOGUE

Darlinghurst Fire Station, Sydney, 2009

'Hey, Bear. What's the ETE?'

'Estimated Time of Eating is about seven.'

I am peeling potatoes at the sink. Don't get me wrong: I'm not doing the cooking because I'm the only girl on shift. It just happens to be my turn. We go in rank, you see, which puts me about halfway down the list. Our boss, the station officer, goes first, then the old fella, better known as the Spy because his surname is Schmidt. He's been in the job forty years and he's been the Spy for about that long too.

I'm 'the Bear'.

I was given the name one night when the boys on my shift were doing door duty. In case you didn't know, that's the serious business of standing at the fire station entrance in front of the truck and watching the world go by, or, more precisely, assessing the female talent that streams past on Friday and Saturday nights in Kings Cross. As a woman, this particular hobby holds about as much interest as watching a kettle boil, but it provides many hours of entertainment for the others, all of whom are male.

So, that particular evening, about a year after I'd started at the station, a hen party came past. (Girls always love firemen; I have always lamented that the same cannot be said for men and female firefighters.) It was about one in the morning and

1

I'd gone to my room to try and get some rest between fire calls; Saturday nights are always busy. I'd been lying down for an hour or so with my eyes closed, trying to endure the painful sound of the girls' shrill laughter and the men on the door flirting with them. When I couldn't stand it a moment longer, I got up and asked them, very politely, if they could be quiet. According to the boys, I gave them a death stare that was frightening enough to stop everything: the flirting, the fun. They said I was grizzly. Then Big Gez pointed out that I got pretty scary when hungry or tired, and from then on I became known as the Bear.

When I've had enough of them all I always go to my room. After the hen night incident, it became known as my cave, and the boys would all warn each other with a smirk that it was only safe to enter if they brought honey and berries with them. Soon, I started finding little bear-related items all around the station: on my ID tag, in my locker and anywhere else they could think of.

Pretty much every firefighter has a nickname; some more flattering than others. All in all, Bear wasn't too bad.

That was the thing about station life. Whatever you did, any minuscule misdemeanour or mildly eccentric habit you had the misfortune to display, someone would pick up on it. And that would be it. It would follow you around everywhere you went.

There was the time I made myself a cup of tea and forgot to offer one to the lads. I returned from a fire call to find that a picture of a bush fire danger-rating scale had appeared on the whiteboard in the mess room, an arrow pointing to 'Extreme'. Underneath was written: 'Tara: Selfometer'. And from then on, whenever I did anything the slightest bit selfish, the scale would pop up again, arrow inevitably slanted to the right.

So here I am, peeling potatoes at the sink, when the Spy with his silver hair and rugged war-torn face comes up to me.

'It'd better not be another salmon patty night, Bear.'

I'll never live that one down. On my first ever cook-up at the station I created some masterful salmon fishcakes, designed to impress, only I made the rookie error of not cooking nearly enough of them so that one of the guys had to go to the takeaway for a chicken burger afterwards.

'I'm still having therapy for that, three years later,' I laugh.

Then the bells at the fire station start to ring, ascending in volume as they always do.

Expecting it to be another false alarm, I turn everything off on the stove and put down my peeler. The automated voice that follows the bells breaks in: 'Pump 4, assist police.'

I walk into the watch-room of the station to get the printout.

'We've got a jumper,' the boss says to me.

It doesn't register at first. Then I realize it's a suicide. The police often call the fire brigade to help clean up the blood.

I take a breath. 'Where is it?'

'The back of the Cross, Springfield Avenue.'

I walk to the turn-out bay, put on my yellow pants, jacket and helmet; and then on to the truck, pull out of the station, lights and sirens on. I've done it a million times before, but this time feels different. There is a tension across my chest. Swallowing is difficult.

We pull up behind the police vehicle. I see the blood.

'Grab the hose, T. Wash it down,' the boss calls.

I walk to the back of the truck, pulling out the hose reel. As I turn, I see a pair of broken glasses on the ground. Then I look up at the window. In my head I see the figure climbing out of it; the body plummeting to the ground; I feel it all, even the instant of regret. Then the impact as it hits the pavement washes through my body.

I stand there frozen, holding the hose. I am taken back to another time, another country, another body …

Adam.

PART ONE

From Five to Three

CHAPTER 1

England, 1976

'Shev ... SHEV ...'

Grunt.

'Shev, which way now?'

'Uh ... uh ... just a minute ...'

Dad reached below his seat and retrieved the map. We were on our way to Suffolk for a family holiday.

'Why didn't you just keep the map out, Shev?'

'Uh ... uh ... well ... um ... let me see ...'

'For God's sake, Shev. Here, let me look!'

Mum leant over, one hand on the wheel, the other reaching for the map. The three of us were quiet in the back, anxious. I was in the middle, being the youngest, in the duff seat where you were in danger of receiving the wrath of Mum. We'd worked out long ago that that was the one place she could get to with her free hand.

I watched the verge of the road draw closer, a corner looming, Mum looking at the map, Dad dithering, and I said nothing.

'All right, Bridget. I can do it!' Dad was still trying to get the map round the right way and Mum was grabbing at it.

'Mum ... Mum!'

I leant forward and yanked the steering wheel. A look of horror on Mum's face, then she grasped hold of the wheel once more and slammed her foot on the brakes. Silence. Then my dad's voice, soft and calm: 'Oh, Bridget, I do wish you wouldn't do that.'

I felt like saying, 'What? You mean kill us all, Dad?' but of course I didn't. I was too scared to. That was the thing: Mum was scary.

Dad used to drive when he first met Mum, if you could call it that, but after two years of driving her car, he still hadn't been able to change the gears. Then, shortly after my elder sister Jo was born, he had an accident while the baby was in the car. That was when Mum put her foot down and stopped him from driving.

Mum and Dad had met in April 1966 at a mutual friend's party full of television producers, academics and writers in a trendy part of North London. They'd seen each other across the room, Dad immediately attracted to the tall, statuesque blonde with blue eyes and a crop of short curly hair. She was wearing a white dress and leant casually on the fireplace. According to Dad, Mum had bowed her head in such a way that indicated she wouldn't be averse to his 'amorous advances', as he put it. He then proceeded to engage her in a conversation about the latest book he was reading, *The Assistant* by Bernard Malamud. He threw in talk of psychoanalysis and psychology as a means of impressing her, somehow managing to extract her phone number. Mum had gushed the next morning to her colleague at the BBC, where she worked as a documentary researcher, about how she'd met this incredibly handsome young Indian academic. She had a thirst for travel and a fascination for India, having been there herself just the year before. She was excited, talking quickly, infected already by the drug of attraction. She was thirty-three years old with a string of relationships behind her and a sense of adventure and curiosity, much to her staid English parents' dismay.

At the time, Mum shared a flat with her best friend, on Gayton Crescent in Hampstead, which was then a fashionable part of London, although not quite as exclusive as it became in later years. When Dad arrived at the flat for their first date, he immediately noticed a copy of *The Assistant* displayed on the mantlepiece. He smiled to himself before whisking my mother off for dinner and a screening of *The Palm Beach Story* at the National Film Theatre. Dad did his best to persuade Mum he should stay the night. My mother giggled as she gently sent him on his way.

From there my mother and father's romance moved quickly. Dad fascinated her with his quirky sense of humour, his intelligent, animated talk and his Indian heritage. He, on the other hand, was drawn to her for her beauty, her energy and her passion for India. They made an attractive couple. Within months Mum was pregnant. My father smiles as he recounts how they became engaged in June of that year at a ball in Oxford. My mother's conservative parents were horrified at the thought of their daughter marrying an Indian man, but that was never going to stop my mother. They married on her thirty-fourth birthday, 6 August 1966, at a small church in Hampstead, the very same church in which our family was to shed an ocean of tears in the years to come.

On the first morning of their honeymoon in Yugoslavia, barely four months after they had met, Dad appeared at the beach wearing a full suit, tie and dress shoes, as well as the hat he'd worn on his wedding day, much to my mother's amused concern. Perhaps it was at this point that she received her first inkling of what she was in for.

We grew up in a terraced house in North London, just down the road from the Royal Free Hospital: my parents, my elder sister Jo, my brother Adam and me, the youngest sibling – just a normal family.

'Mum! Mum …'

'What is it, Tara?'

'Jo stuck a peanut up Adam's nose. Now she can't get it down.'

'Ask your father, please. I'm doing the washing.'

Mum had her hands in a tub in the kitchen sink, wringing out an endless line of clothes. According to Mum, we couldn't afford a washing machine. Dad was in the living room in his customary position: sunk deep into his armchair, nose in a book.

'Dad!'

No answer

'Daaaaad!'

Still no answer

'Daaaaaaad!' I screamed at the top of my voice.

A subdued grunt emanated from somewhere far away in the armchair where my father resided.

'Oh, for Christ's sake!' Mum muttered in exasperation, grabbing a tea towel to dry her hands and following me into the backyard, only to find my sister attempting to prod a bamboo rod up my brother's nose in a vain attempt to remove said peanut – clearly the best implement for this delicate operation.

'Joanna! What in hell's name are you doing?' Mum grabbed the bamboo stick from my sister's hand and firmly whacked her on the bottom.

'Ouch!' My sister squealed. 'How come he never gets hit?' she snarled at my brother as my mother attended to the peanut lodged firmly up Adam's nose. I merely stood chewing my bottom lip anxiously.

Mum was the law enforcer and the backbone of our family. She did everything at speed. As a young child I had to run to keep up with her purposeful strides down the road. Her hands were strong, tough and hard-working. Hands that you wouldn't want to mess with. My father's, on the other hand, were clumsy but exquisitely soft and malleable and made you want to hold them. They said a lot about his slow-moving, pacifist nature. Of course these dichotomies made for interesting one-sided arguments, which generally involved my mum screaming and shouting and my father muttering quietly in his most perfect English accent, 'I do wish you wouldn't shout, Bridget', which only fuelled my mother's fury.

Mum insisted we went on family camping holidays. Unfortunately, my father hated camping, particularly after a trip that involved us arriving at a deserted campsite in the north of Scotland during a wild storm. Mum and we three kids battled with the tent as it billowed in the gale-force winds, each of us clinging on to a tent pole to ensure the whole contraption didn't end up in the Irish Sea. I was petrified. Dad, meanwhile, walked off to find the nearest shop, disappearing for what seemed like hours, only to return bearing a packet of Penguin biscuits. His answer to all discontent was chocolate, which we all thought was fantastic and a perfectly valid reason to love him more. Needless to say this habit drove my mother crazy.

So it would seem we were just a normal, marginally angst-ridden family, except for one thing that I have no recollection of: my father suffered a nervous breakdown when I was two. In fact, Dad had suffered some form of mental illness for most of his life, the impact of which I had no idea of at the time.

'Daddy ...' Dad was sitting quietly in his armchair, eyes open but vacant.

'Yes, lovey,' he said quietly.

'Daddy, can I have a cuddle?' I said, looking up at him and placing my hands on his lap.

'Not now, lovey, Daddy's resting,' he said with a gentle fatigue in his voice.

I kept looking at him, wide-eyed, craving his love and affection. Why wouldn't Daddy cuddle me? I chewed my lip, unsure what to do, eventually deciding to scramble onto his lap in the hope of finding comfort for us both. Still my father sat motionless, entombed in a glass case which I could not penetrate. I nestled my head into his chest, desperate to get close, but my father remained lost in his own world. Finally I used all my strength to awkwardly lift his arm up so that I could place it around me in a kind of makeshift half-cuddle.

It seemed unsatisfying for us both, so after a short time I clambered down off my father's lap, running into the kitchen in search of my mother.

Mum, as always was busy. She appeared to be cleaning while also wallpapering the house single-handed.

'Oh shit!' I heard her mutter as she hung a piece of wallpaper up the wrong way.

It didn't seem like the right time to ask for a cuddle, so I decided I would help Mum instead by drying the dishes. I liked being Mum's little helper, only I had a habit of being clumsy. Just when I most wanted to avoid Mum's wrath a plate seemed to jump out of my hands, and smashed into a thousand pieces on the floor. I stared at it, horrified, before scarpering into the living room and taking refuge behind the nearest chair. I knew Mum would have heard the crash. I could hear her footsteps getting closer.

'What on earth was that?' she huffed. I cowered.

Eventually she located me curled up behind the chair. Her anger dissolved, replaced by a look of horror as the realization dawned on her that her six-year-old daughter was terrified of her. She cocooned me in her arms, rocking and stroking me. I basked in the safety. At last – a golden moment of affection.

My sister ruled the roost between us siblings. She was like a child version of Mum, strong-willed, somewhat bossy and a little bit scary. Underneath it all, though, she was affectionate and caring, it was just that Adam and I didn't see that side of her very often. We simply feared her and strove endlessly for her approval.

The saliva game involved my sister pinning either me or my brother down with her knees, trapping us, enabling her to lean over the unfortunate younger sibling while she commenced the tortuous exercise of extending a long globule of saliva from her mouth. I would see it coming, squealing and squirming as the thread of spit grew ever more tenuous. Intense fear gripped me. God forbid that saliva should actually touch me or worse, enter my open mouth.

Ad and I tended to stick together during these games, except for the times when it seemed more important for our own self-preservation that we remain on our sister's side and generally champion all her actions. There was one occasion we were on holiday with our family friends who, unfortunately for Adam, had three daughters, so of course I sided with Jo and them when she suggested that Adam put out the fire we had going by peeing on it – as he was the only one who had the 'reach'.

On one particular family holiday the three of us dug a huge hole in the sand. Jo cajoled Adam into getting in it while she and I filled it up with sand. We were all having fun until the sand neared his neck and he realized he couldn't move. I watched horrified as his infectious vibrant smile morphed into a look of intense panic. Jo didn't seem to feel the urgency that I felt. She was amused by the sight of only my brother's head popping out of the sand until, that is, Adam started shouting and we began digging frantically to extricate him. My heart was pounding. I loved Adam. That look on his face came to haunt me in later years.

Even from an early age Adam and I looked out for each other. He wrote letters to me whenever I went away.

Dear Fuzzy,

How are you? We are all well. I haven't noticed any letters from you in the post yet, but sure some are on the way, aren't they? Hint hint! I bet you've spent all your money already, on sweets no doubt! Oh yes, how's the riding going? I can almost imagine you carrying the pony instead of it carrying you! Do you realize I haven't seen you for: let me see, eleven whole days – what bliss! No, not really I'm looking forward to seeing my little sister again. It's been so quiet while you've been away. No pattering of feet in the morning and no little head popping out of the bed covers in the morning. Anyway, we're all (not) missing you (only a joke) and are looking forward to seeing the curly-haired baby (in other words – you) again.
Love from Ad xxx

PS Please dance with someone at the disco.

We used to play this game that involved one of us climbing onto the other's shoulders so that we could reach and cling to a small bit of cornice that lined an archway between the living and dining area in our home. We only had the very ends of our fingertips to grip with so it was a precarious manoeuvre. If I was on my brother's shoulders, I would be left to dangle from my fingertips while he ran up and down the room as many times as possible until I screamed to be picked up, whereupon Adam would stand underneath me, once more taking my weight on his shoulders. Adam and I trusted each other implicitly; not once did either of us allow the other one to fall.

Generally, the three of us got along. We were happy, blissfully unaware of the mental illness that shrouded my father in a dark cloak, threatening to engulf him.

CHAPTER 2

My father was the first of three sons, born in 1931 in Burhpur, a small, bustling village in northern India. He always smiles when he recalls those first six years of his life in the family home. His eyes glaze over as he retreats into the haven of his childhood, gently nodding with a soft fondness for his treasured memories. His face is blurred by a hazy sadness; his idyllic home and family are long since a distant, faded reality.

My father doesn't recall his mother acting oddly.

'That's nonsense,' he says when his brother mentions that their mother would talk to herself and often behave strangely. 'She was just dealing with the normal stresses of motherhood,' Dad says confidently.

But when Dad was six his father decided to pack the family up on a boat bound for England, ostensibly to secure a good education for his sons, but also in the hope that the change would be good for his wife. He had been educated in the UK, the son of a wealthy and eminent Indian lawyer and advisor to the Congress Party. Legend has it that Nehru once stayed at the family property in India.

My grandfather secured a job in England and then sent for his wife and sons to join him. So, in 1937, my father, his mother and his younger brother were herded onto a rickety old train bound for the port of Bombay, where they began their six-week journey. Despite being only six years old at the time, certain images from the trip remain imprinted in my father's memory: the incredibly blue water as they sailed into Malta, a random lifeboat exercise in the Bay of Biscay and the brightly coloured bunting that greeted them as they sailed into England.

'Look, Maataaji! Look what they did for us!' he squealed excitedly in Hindi, pointing at the bunting, completely unaware of the coronation of George VI, or indeed who George VI was.

The family lived in Catford in South London, where my grandfather had a medical practice. Soon after arriving, my father came running down the stairs and bumped into a young English lady whom his father had employed to tutor his sons. He started talking in Hindi. Why didn't she answer his questions? She was speaking in a strange way. It didn't make sense. He wandered into the bathroom, peering puzzledly at the toilet, taken aback by the rushing water when he pulled the chain. Funny how everything just disappeared, he mused.

It wasn't long after the family arrived in England that the war broke out. My grandfather was called up to serve in the medical corps in the Indian army. Convinced his family would be safer out of London, he moved them to Basingstoke, but they were isolated there and Dad's mother began to crumble under the stress. Then a bomb exploded in a church right next to their house and she panicked, screaming at her kids to put on their ill-fitting gas masks. When my father recalls that day he closes his eyes and scrunches up his face as if by doing so he might halt the memory in its tracks. Even now he will exit the room when a bottle of champagne is opened. He wears earplugs during storms, and a balloon bursting leaves him cowering in his chair like a frightened child. As kids we thought it hilarious that Dad was frightened of balloons, teasing him endlessly.

Perhaps it was the bomb incident that tipped my grand-mother over the edge, for one Sunday morning in 1943 my father awoke to find his mother in an agitated frenzy, howling, incoherent words streaming endlessly from her mouth, eyes wild. Frightened, he ran up the road to find a local dentist the family knew. Various doctors and seemingly important people arrived at the house: the general consensus was that Dad's mother was suffering from a nervous breakdown.

My father and his two brothers watched helplessly as their mother was whisked away to a psychiatric hospital, labelled as crazy and later diagnosed with paranoid schizophrenia. Welfare services were called in, taking the three young boys to the nearest orphanage. Dad recalls with terrifying clarity his first night of what he describes bitterly as a living hell. He lay awake, twelve years old, staring at the dark ceiling of the dormitory, trying to block out the stifled sobs of others, haunted by the look in his mother's eyes, the sound of her howls. He felt he was drowning, cast out to sea without a life raft, nothing solid to reach out for, engulfed by a sea of uncertainty. What would happen to him and his brothers? Would he ever see his mother again? What was wrong with her? Why was she acting so strangely?

Then one day he found some old leather-bound books hidden in a cupboard in the orphanage. As he began to read, the words took him to another world, far away from his shattered reality. He read and re-read those books over and over, a haven from the hell. When ensconced in his books he was safe.

Mrs Harding lived up the road from the Lal family. Her husband was working overseas so she was at home alone with her young daughter. She used to see the Indian family that lived in the neighbourhood on occasion. News spread that the boys were in the orphanage, so she set about arranging a visit. She stepped into the grounds of the overcrowded building, immediately shocked by the scene that greeted her eyes as she scanned the sea of white faces in search of dark skin. Her eyes came to rest on my father, sitting quietly cross-legged in a corner, clutching a book, his brothers huddled nearby. Her heart melted the moment she set eyes on the boys with their huge, endearing brown eyes. In that moment she vowed to take them home with her, shower them with love and save them from a life of institutionalized hell. She fostered all three of the boys during the war.

Increasingly, Dad immersed himself in books. Reading provided an escape from the confusion of his short childhood; reading became his passion. The books helped him cope.

After the war, in 1945, my grandfather decided to take his wife and two youngest sons back to India to look after the family property. Having everything worked out, he left Dad with Mrs Harding in England so he could finish school, follow in his footsteps and become a doctor. His youngest son would also be a doctor, but Shambhuji, the middle son, would remain in India and enter the Indian army. And so it was: the three sons diligently followed the paths that had been laid out for them. Three years later, my grandfather returned to England with his wife and youngest son and set up a medical practice in the Old Kent Road in London, while his wife ricocheted in and out of psychiatric hospitals. My father was twenty-two when his mother finally died after succumbing to tuberculosis. No one told him she had passed away, for he too was in hospital suffering from the very same disease. Only a year later did he learn of her death upon his own release from hospital.

My father first suffered some form of mental illness as a teenager, although what his symptoms were I don't know. He was later variously diagnosed with schizoaffective disorder, bipolar disorder and depression. Driven by his mother's illness, the youngest son, my uncle Samarthji, went on to become a highly respected professor of psychiatry in Canada, focusing much of his research on schizophrenia. Recent research from his institute in the field of epigenetics has revealed how genes can be 'painted' or 'coloured' by environmental exposure. Emotional and physical triggers are superimposed on our unique genetic imprint to determine the expression of those genes in any individual.

I have often asked myself whether my father's psychological struggles were the result of a genetic trait passed on to him from his mother or a product of the trauma he endured during his childhood. I could ask the same about my brother.

❖

My father completed his medical training and became a doctor. We kids found this hilarious as my father's answer to all ailments was invariably 'take an aspirin and go to bed'.

Thankfully, for the welfare of all, following his intern year, my father went against Indian tradition by ignoring his father's wishes and abandoned his medical career to study for a PhD in neurophysiology.

When Dad spoke about his research his whole body became animated, eyes shining as he described one neuron passing a unique message to another, encoding some meaningful piece of information in a single nerve impulse, a beautiful, seamless flow of information from one medium to another. In those moments of heartfelt engagement Dad was stripped of his sadness and regret, affording us a rare glimpse of the enigmatic, passionate, real Dr Lal.

When Dad was engaged with a subject, he could be very funny. He cracked himself up every time he told us his favourite joke. It always began the same way: 'Have you heard the one about the absent-minded professor?'

'Yes, Dad!' we all chorused in mock boredom. At which point my father would continue regardless.

'Well, the professor was walking down the road, thinking of his work, when he realized he couldn't remember the way home. So he stopped to ask a little girl who was playing in the street for directions.

'"Excuse me, little girl."' My dad would put on his absent-minded professor voice. '"Do you know the way to 115 Constantine Road?"'

'And the little girl replied, "You're funny, Daddy!"'

At which point my father began hiccupping with laughter, which in turn made us all fall about in hysterics.

Our house was filled with Dad's books. Every conceivable nook or cranny had a book in it. Books were lined up horizontally and when that became unfeasible they were piled vertically. It drove Mum crazy. When we went on a two-week holiday, Dad took twenty books with him and read them all. I never could understand how he did that or how, even more impressively, he could recall every detail of each book he'd read.

I could always tell when Dad was depressed. He would sit in his comfortable brown armchair that had become moulded to his body over the years, but he wouldn't have a book on his knee. Instead he would sit motionless with his eyes closed. As I said, I cannot recollect his first nervous breakdown, but as an adult I look back and wonder how it affected us all. I have often felt that there is something that blocks me, a memory perhaps that I can't quite reach. When, in my thirties, I retraced my childhood, images came to me of myself as a toddler. There was one scene in particular, where I peered round a door to see my father sitting in the corner of a bare hospital room, rocking back and forth, eyes clenched shut. I wanted to go to him, put my arms around him, but I was whisked away. Was this a real memory? I wonder.

My memories of being older, about ten or eleven, are much clearer. I remember Mum taking me to visit Dad in the psychiatric hospital. I was nervous. I didn't want to tell anyone that my dad was in a 'mental' hospital. To my surprise and relief it seemed quite a nice place, not cold and sterile as I had imagined. But still it felt weird. I looked around thinking, *Everyone must be nuts in here … but my dad isn't nuts.*

They took all his razor blades away from him. I had no idea what this meant at the time. Only that Dad found it annoying as he didn't like electric shavers. All I knew was that when Dad was in hospital we went to visit him, and that was just part of life.

I scribbled in my diary:

Dad's depressed. I hate it when Dad's depressed because he's so quiet and I always think it's my fault.

CHAPTER 3

Mum was tough. She did what she had to do. She cooked and cleaned, drove and shopped, did all our washing by hand. She was tall and strong with broad shoulders and slim hips. I'm built just like her. She worked hard in her new career as a social worker; she ran the family budget and somehow found time to love and cuddle us. In short, she did everything in her power to keep our family together throughout my father's illness and his subsequent inability to cope.

I was completely unaware of the load she was carrying. I remember seeing her cry only once. It was the day that Jo and Adam broke Mum's sculpture, a figure of a girl with blonde hair, standing on some rocks by the ocean. It was called *Sea Breezes*, and Mum's father had given it to her, saying that it reminded him of her. We knew it was her favourite thing; she'd told us to be careful of it often enough. My sister and brother were always fighting. Snooker balls were a favourite, and on this occasion the black ball missed its target. We watched, horrified, as the sculpture toppled from the mantlepiece and smashed into a million pieces on the floor. We stared at each other in silence, before the fighting started again: Jo and Adam arguing over whose fault it was and who was going to tell Mum. I felt an intense relief that I hadn't been the one to throw the offending ball. We knew that the culprit would be in for a hiding. But, as it turned out, we got worse than that. Mum didn't hit us; she cried.

21

❉

Dad and I lived in fear of Mum. On one particular Saturday morning my father had been coerced to come to do the weekly food shop at Sainsbury's with Mum and me. We queued in the usual mayhem of Saturday morning shoppers with our trolley full of food. The young check-out girl announced, 'That's fifty-five pounds and twenty-five pence, please.'

'Don't be ridiculous,' Mum exclaimed, with some force, staring at the girl. 'You've overcharged me.'

Dad and I stared down at our feet.

'Bridget, just leave it, I'm sure it's fine,' Dad pointed out meekly.

'You'll have to run it all through again,' Mum pronounced, completely ignoring Dad's comment. The check-out girl rolled her eyes but proceeded to run the entire shop through the till once more as the queue of tutting, harassed mothers behind us grew ever longer. Twenty sets of eyes glared at us. Dad and I stood still in mortified silence. At the end of it all, we'd been overcharged by the grand total of one pound twenty.

'See!' my mother exclaimed triumphantly. Of course, my father and I would have happily paid the extra and saved the embarrassment.

Only once did I witness my father retaliate in an argument with my mother. It happened in the car, when my parents were going through their usual pattern of car-guments. This time, though, when Mum unleashed her routine verbal tirade on Dad, something snapped in him.

'Stop ... Stop the car!'

My mother, shocked by the uncharacteristic force in his voice, put her foot on the brakes. Almost before the car had come to a halt, my father opened the passenger door and stepped out, clutching his book. 'That's it, Bridget. I've had enough.'

He walked off purposefully, even though he had no idea of where he was or in what direction he was heading. The three of us sat wide-eyed in the back.

'Daddy, please come back!' I squealed.

Mum was silent for a while as she contemplated how best to deal with this curious change in her husband's behaviour. Then she got out of the car and apologized to him, an action that was as uncharacteristic of her as rebellion was of him.

I know Mum had a tender side but she rarely showed it. She could be very funny too. I remember her taking us by surprise as she hid behind a wall during one of our family holidays. We wondered where she'd gone until we saw her head appearing slowly from behind the stone bricks, first a few stray curls of blonde hair, then her eyes, bright and cheeky, followed by her nose and lips, all her features contorted into a cartoon-like caricature, leaving only her head visible.

We kids giggled, desperate for more of our mischievous mum. She paused briefly before sinking slowly once more behind the wall, waiting for a minute before repeating the manoeuvre with another stupid un-Mum-like face, ending the whole show by walking up and down imaginary stairs as per Marcel Marceau, which of course caused us all to fall about with laughter.

I loved to see Mum laugh, but increasingly those rare glimpses of lightness became swamped by the burden of Dad's illness and the strains of family life. There always seemed to be too much to do.

Then things got a whole lot worse. Mum got sick. I was eight when she found a lump in her left breast. She didn't do anything about it immediately. She was frightened. My Mum, frightened? It didn't seem possible. She was too strong to be scared.

She sent us to stay at my aunt and uncle's place in Northumberland while she had her mastectomy. I sat and ever so carefully made her a Get Well card, drawing little feet all the way across the envelope, tracing a convoluted journey back home.

Did I understand what it meant? No, not really. I knew Mum was ill and I knew she had cancer. I knew people died of cancer. But Mum was okay; she was getting better.

✳

We used to visit her at the Royal Free Hospital when she was having chemotherapy. I would help bake cakes for her and make cups of tea, but I had no real understanding of what was going on. I just knew I should be good and not cause trouble. Mum was ill, and that meant we had to try to help her; so was Dad, but he didn't *look* ill. Nothing in his appearance told us he was unwell, so we couldn't understand. We didn't know how to help him.

One evening when Mum was in hospital I was at home with Dad. He was working and I was on the couch in front of the television.

'Tara, it's time to go and see your mother,' Dad muttered from the other end of the room, where he sat at his desk. I rolled my eyes. *Dallas* was on at 8pm. It was getting really exciting. We were getting close to finding out who shot JR Ewing. I'd miss it if I went to the hospital.

'I'm going to stay here, Dad. *Dallas* is on.'

'Are you sure, Tara?'

'Yep, I'll go tomorrow.' *Phew*, I thought as I nestled into the couch, eyes glued to the television.

Later that night Dad returned from the hospital.

'Your mother's upset, Tara.'

'Why?' I asked, even though I knew the answer.

'Because you didn't go and visit her.'

'Oh,' I said, feeling guilty. It had seemed so important to watch *Dallas*. So I baked a cake and took it up to the hospital the next day. Mum didn't say anything, but I saw the disappointment in her eyes. From that day on I knew I was selfish.

I can recall random events through the course of Mum's illness, yet my memories have no emotion attached to them. When Mum had to get a hairpiece, all I remember was thinking that it was way too grey for her. I thought it looked terrible and I was embarrassed by it. It never occurred to me how traumatic it must have been for Mum to lose her hair – or her breast, for that matter.

She got a new swimming costume that had an extra piece of material to cover the side where she'd had the mastectomy. Mum told me that it would look less obvious if the costume had the extra material only on the one side. I thought it looked weird. Especially as, being Mum, she had sewn the fabric piece into the costume herself: fuchsia pink with a white floral pattern, although her costume was navy blue.

Those are the things I remember. The material signs of her illness. Not the symptoms or the trauma.

CHAPTER 4

I was always worried about being in the way or being a nuisance. I saw the burden on my mum and, not knowing how else to help, I shrank. I did everything possible to avoid conflict, to avoid being seen.

At school, I was the ultimate goody-goody. I never did anything wrong or drew attention to myself. When a teacher praised me in class for being picked to train with one of the country's top athletics coaches I tried to hide my head under the desk. The further I shrank the safer I felt. And the only way I knew how to help was to be good.

There had to be a cost for the load my mother had been carrying and continued to carry. She was not only a mother, but also a father, a worker and a patient. So many things sucked the life from her, and the space for tenderness became ever smaller.

She battled to stay alive. She turned vegan, and suddenly we were eating raw courgettes and spinach salads. One day I ran into the living room and found her perched on a meditation stool. I just wanted to know where my T-shirt was. She drank carrot juice three times a day until her fingertips started to turn orange and the man in the grocery shop at the end of our road asked if we had a donkey. I just thought it was weird.

It was an irony that my father wanted his life to end while my mother did everything possible to keep hers going.

*

As hard as Mum fought, she couldn't stop the cancer and it returned as liver metastases.

We went to Wales on a family holiday and, instead of camping, we stayed in a place that provided meals for us. *Wow*, I thought. *This is fantastic.*

As always, Mum had driven us there.

'I think we'll stop and have a rest.' She turned to us in the back. 'How would you like a milkshake?'

'Yes please, Mum!'

This is getting better and better, I thought. We were never allowed milkshakes.

In the service station Mum disappeared into the bathroom. We finished our milkshakes and there was still no sign of her. Slowly my excitement drained away and was replaced by a feeling of anxiety.

'Why's Mum taking so long?'

'Your mother is not feeling so well,' Dad said.

'Oh.'

Dad didn't say anything more but he looked worried and that made me scared. We sat in silence.

After an hour or so, Mum reappeared. It was then that I saw how jaundiced and bloated she had become, how thin and brittle her hair. However much she tried, there was no way now that she could hide her illness from us. It was draining the life from her in front of our eyes.

We got back in the car and continued the journey. Mum didn't say anything about what had happened. She never complained, not once through her entire illness. When she had found out that her cancer had returned, she sat down with us and talked about death for the first time. I was twelve years old and all the time I was thinking: What do you mean? You're having treatment; you're getting better. Other people die from cancer but not you. You're my mum. You can't die. You just can't.

I went to school the next day and broke down in tears. They called my dad to pick me up but he was ill himself, unable to do anything for anybody. I went to bed that night and sobbed.

Mum heard me and came into my room. She tried to comfort me but she could not reassure me of the one thing I needed to hear: that she would always be there.

At that moment I realized for the first time that maybe it wasn't going to be okay; that maybe, just maybe, the world wasn't a safe place after all. I saw the word 'loss' on the horizon and I tried to push it away behind a cloud.

I only witnessed my mum's despair once in the whole time she was ill. My father called us all into their bedroom, where my mum lay curled up on her side. Dad sat next to Mum on the edge of the bed, slumped, resting his hand on her shoulder. I'd never seen my mother like that before. She looked vulnerable. It frightened me.

'Your mother needs to talk to you all,' my father said softly.

'I think I'm dying. I don't want to leave you …' My mother's voice wavered, trailing off.

Our responses said a lot about our personalities.

My sister was strong and practical. 'Mum, you have to believe you're getting better. Be strong and fight it.'

My brother stood slightly away from the bed, quietly internalizing it all.

I simply curled up next to Mum and cried.

CHAPTER 5

The phone rang when I was playing a board game with my best friend, Kitty. It was Dad. He sounded different.

'Uh, Tara ... um ... I think you should come to the hospital to see your mother.'

Kitty and I walked up the road in silence, two thirteen-year-old girls. I knew; Kitty knew. We didn't speak, but I had a heavy feeling of foreboding that would become hauntingly familiar to me in the ensuing years, a backpack on my soul.

At the junction, I said goodbye to Kitty and continued up the road to the hospital. I was feeling nervous.

My mother lay in her hospital bed, semi-conscious, drowsy. A nurse drew the curtains around us and I stood beside the bed, distant, watching. Mum's speech was slurred and she fought to keep her eyes from closing. Still she tried to comfort me. I sat helpless, a blank mind, only tears to speak the language of my soul, for she was leaving me, slipping slowly and helplessly away.

The weekend Mum died Adam was on Dartmoor, participating in the Ten Tors event with his school team. The organizers had to locate the team and then airlift Adam to London by helicopter so that he could get to the hospital in time. He was fifteen years old. The three of us, Adam, Jo and I, went to the hospital. I didn't realize we were there to say goodbye. Or maybe I did but didn't want to, or didn't know how.

That night I awoke, panicking. I couldn't sleep. Darkness was closing in. What if Mum dies before I have time to see her? I have to see her one more time. I have to say goodbye. I have to …

I got out of bed, agitated. I don't remember who was there or who took me to the hospital. My recollection of this time is so confused.

I entered the hospital through Accident and Emergency. It seemed different at night, quiet, subdued, surreal, as if it were beckoning death. I do not remember saying goodbye, yet I must have done so, otherwise why would I have gone to the hospital in the dead of night? It seems cruel that I cannot recall the one moment I most wish to hold on to.

Adam remembered saying goodbye to Mum. Much later, I found a scrap of paper, torn from an A4 lined notebook. On one side was a series of maths equations:

$$x/30 + x = 7/13$$
$$13x = 7(30 + x)$$
$$13x = 210 + 7x$$
$$6x = 210$$
$$x = 210/6$$

On the other side, in Adam's familiar spindly handwriting:

For all those I love …

The peace of love for my mother

I came and watched; my only contribution to a dying body. In my mind was a deathly emptiness, a tear of confused emotion compared to the reality of the love falling from my eyes. The peace that she held was contradicted by the hoarse roughness of her fight for her very own fleeing life. There before me lay the scaffold of my soul, the support upon which my own life had grown.

His words captured the moment of disconnection so eloquently. One brutal cutting of the cord that binds you to life, the cord that connects you not only to the one you love, but also to the world around you and to yourself. When slashed it leaves you flailing, floating, ungrounded, disconnected. Two entwined souls separating, brutally wrenched from each other's grip. Therein lay the foundations of grief, captured in an instant yet valid for a lifetime.

I woke the next morning to find that Mum had passed away in the early hours. Her brother Michael had been with her when she died. Dad wasn't coping. Once again, I don't remember who told me she was gone: was it my uncle, my sister, my aunt? I only remember my reaction to the news.

'I'm glad.'

At thirteen years old I thought this was the mature thing to say. Mum was not suffering any more and I should be happy for that. How could I be glad that I had lost my mother? I didn't know how I was supposed to act or to be. When would I be allowed to smile again? What were you supposed to do when your mother died? No one told me that.

The days after Mum's death are hazy, blurred and lacking in continuity. I don't remember the pain, only random meaningless instants in time. Like Suzy, my aunt and uncle's dog lying growling at the base of our stairs, making it impossible for anyone to pass. I was only concerned about acting grown-up, wearing something nice to the funeral. How come it was okay for Jo to wear red to the funeral, but not for me to wear electric blue? What was the difference?

I only remember two things from the funeral (and I wasn't wearing my electric-blue top). Firstly, I recall trying not to giggle as I heard my aunt, who is tone deaf, singing next to me. I was supposed to be sad and my suppressed laughter sat awkwardly within the grief. I berated myself. Secondly, I remember the crematorium. I stood and watched as the coffin moved along the conveyor belt through the curtains and into the fire. I wanted to run to it, to reach out and pull it back. I looked desperately around at all the people. Why did no one stop it? Couldn't they see that she was leaving, that I wasn't ready to say goodbye? Why are you all just standing there doing and saying nothing? I screamed a silent *'Noooo ... come back, don't leave'*. I wanted to run to it, to her, to hold on to her, to go with her into the fire. Anything but lose her. But no sound came from my mouth, no movement from my body. I remained paralysed, locked in emotional chains, a straitjacket of fear. I stood and watched, helpless, yearning, grief-stricken.

CHAPTER 6

Dad was acting strangely. He was the most joyous I'd ever seen him, possessed by a manic happiness. He talked incessantly, ranting and excited. He didn't seem like Dad at all. It was as if Mum's decline was the best thing that ever happened to him, filling him with superhuman energy and charisma. He was planning a new life of restaurants and freedom; how to spend his money. I had never seen him like this.

The mania could tip into paranoia. I remember one day sitting at the top of the stairs, hugging my legs, chin resting on my knees, listening to Dad's voice, which was raised in a howl.

'They've been following me. I'm telling you, they are! They think I don't know but I do!'

Then the confused voice of our neighbour, 'Who's been following you, Shev?'

'They've been tapping my phone. They're all in it. They're listening.'

'No one's following you, Shev.'

I went back to my room, feeling sick and confused. Later I found out that this paranoid fancy that he was being followed by Russian spies was just one in a series. Jo, being seventeen, heard much more: he had told her that he was going to move to the country and become a reclusive alcoholic (strange, as he didn't really drink) and that he was going to sell the house for virtually nothing because 'it didn't matter' and would give the proceeds to an Indian charity.

When Dad's brother came over from Canada for the funeral he took one look at my father and immediately had him admitted to a psychiatric hospital. Over the next year Dad was allowed to come home for weekends at first, which became longer stays over time.

Mum had done everything in her power to organize things so that we were supported after her death. We were all minors and she didn't want us separated or looked after by strangers. She had been frightened for our future, knowing that my father would be unlikely to cope. None of us knew or could possibly guess how he would react when she died.

She had arranged for us to have family therapy. I found the sessions weird, as if the therapist, a large lady with a bun on top of her head, was trying to invade our family. She was adamant that the three of us should be farmed out separately to different families. I was to go to my best friend Kitty's family; Adam was to go to our next-door neighbour; Jo was to go to a family that lived round the corner with whom we used to go on holiday.

I remember being asked if I wanted to go and live with Kitty and her family. I didn't know what to say, didn't want to offend anyone, but inside I screamed '*No*'. It wasn't going to be the same. They weren't my family. I just wanted *my* family. I wanted my family to be together again like it used to be. Why couldn't it be the way it was before? But I said nothing.

Thankfully, not long before she died, Mum had asked her brother Michael and his wife Margaret to take care of us in the event that Dad wasn't able to. Mum was close to my aunt Margaret. They had been friends for years, and in the months leading up to my mother's death they had spoken every day.

Although my aunt and uncle became our legal guardians they lived in Newcastle, several hours away, and had their own children to care for. Luckily for us, though, they fought tooth and nail for the three of us to stay together, even taking the case to the High Court.

At last, a plan was made. As no one knew how long Dad would be in hospital, and as Jo was seventeen and a minor, it was decided that a room in our house would be rented to a lodger and we would go to our neighbours for dinner every night. Wednesday evenings I would spend with Kitty's family.

Jo often chose to have dinner with her boyfriend's family. At the time I couldn't understand why she didn't want to be with me and Adam. I wanted us all to be together, all of the time.

Eventually Dad started coming out of hospital for the weekends, but remnants of his mania remained. When he was home he wanted to eat out every night, which felt strange and uncomfortable to us after a lifetime of being rationed to one treat a week by Mum: an éclair at Lindy's tearooms on a Saturday morning.

One morning he turned to Jo at the breakfast table. 'I know what we'll do. We'll have a dinner party!' He was talking fast, his eyes sparkling. 'Joanna, I'll need you to host it for me.'

'But Dad, I've got an exam on Monday.' Jo was doing her A-levels.

'We'll invite everyone we know and get a caterer in. Adam and Tara can serve drinks.'

'But Dad, do you think it's a good idea?'

'I'll wear my black velvet jacket. Which shirt and tie, I wonder? How about the lilac shirt with the pink tie?'

Dad had his dinner party during one of his interludes from the hospital, and he did wear his black velvet suit with the lilac shirt and fluorescent pink tie. Everyone smiled politely, drank wine and was merry. Dad went back into hospital the next day.

Was I frightened of his madness? Was I relieved that he seemed happy? Was I angry that he should be like this when Mum had just died? I don't know.

In the end, he remained in hospital for nearly a year. I remember visiting him there, walking over the manicured lawns to the reception desk, everything being so quiet. Then down the corridor to my father's room. Peering through the glass panel in the door, seeing him sitting on the edge of the bed with his back to me, hunched over.

I remember feeling scared as I approached the bed, suddenly unsure of exactly who was sitting there. The last time I had seen him he had been ecstatic, thrilled with the library of new books he had bought.

'Dad? It's me.'

No response.

'Dad. It's me.'

He looked up at me with hollow eyes, without a hint of recognition or love in them. I leant over to kiss him on the cheek, tried to hug him, willing him to respond. There was a pause, then Dad slowly lifted his arm. It was as if it had been weighed down by a landslide of mud. He patted me gently on the back.

'How are you, Dad?' I tried to smile, but his eyes were looking down at his feet. Then he closed them, retreating into himself again.

'I've been at school, Dad. I won the long jump at the London Schools Athletics Championship. They put a piece in the paper, but they spelt my name wrong ... Tara Hall.'

His voice when he spoke was so quiet I could hardly hear it. 'Well done, lovey.'

I went home and pulled out the white envelope my mother had left me before she died. She had written letters to each of us, wanting us to have something to keep, to hold on to after her death. I held the sacred letter in my hand, staring at my name scrawled in my mother's handwriting. A stray tear escaped my eye, tumbling down my cheek. Ever so carefully, I opened the envelope, unfolding the letter. Now the tears fell freely, threatening to smudge the very words in which I searched so desperately for answers. I read my letter over and over, grasping for my mother's love, searching the words on the page for the safety of her arms around me.

Tara, my love,

I hope it will be a long, long time before you read this letter, but I wanted to write each of you a letter to keep for yourselves to remember your old mum. Darling, I do feel I have let you down so badly and have been able to share so little of your life with you. You will miss me – or I suppose you will – but when you have recovered from the initial shock and sadness I am sure you will all be able to help each other because I know how much you care for one another. Dad will, I know, need lots of help, but I know you will give him that help and give him lots of cuddles.

I wanted so much to see you grow up, get married and have children – the things that any mother wants – but alas it has not been so. But whatever you do in life, darling, I want you first of all to be happy, secondly to lead a useful and caring life and thirdly to marry and have children eventually, because I know they will give you much pleasure in the way that you have all done for me.

I sat curled up on my bed, craving more, more wisdom, more love, more affection, more help. *Where are you, Mum? I need you. Please come back …*

The words swilled around my head in an endless unanswered quest for comfort. It was a lot to expect: the wisdom and lessons of a lifetime in one letter. I often think how each of us was affected by the words she wrote in those letters.

My letter wasn't signed. Our family therapist pointed that out. Adam's was, Jo's was, mine wasn't. Up until that point, the letter had given me some comfort. But in that instant, the comfort morphed into angst: I was an afterthought. Had she finished the letter? Was it a sign that she didn't love me as much as she loved Adam or Jo? What more had she wanted to say? What vital piece of love or guidance had I missed?

In the ensuing years I would often unfold my sacred letter, looking for answers and love at those times when the world seemed to offer me none.

CHAPTER 7

A year after Mum died, Dad came home from hospital. Physically he was present, but mentally he remained absent, hanging by a tenuous emotional thread. It was as if he were in a darkly tinted bubble that rendered him inaccessible to intimacy, the thing I most craved.

It was a struggle for him to survive each day, let alone support a family or run a household. Living with him was hard. We didn't know how to care for him any more than he knew how to care for us.

Six months after Dad came home, Jo went to study at Norwich University, leaving the three of us to fumble on blindly, learning how to live again. I ironed Dad's shirts because that was what Mum did. I cooked, because that was what Mum did. I did the washing because that was what Mum did.

A year after Mum died, I started menstruating. I was fourteen. No one had ever explained how to use a tampon. I bought a pack of ten and spent an hour in the bathroom trying to figure out how to insert one. I started getting frantic, wondering why everyone else seemed to manage while I couldn't. Maybe there was something wrong with me? On the tenth tampon, I finally figured it out.

I started smoking, just to try to fit in, despite having regularly chastised Adam and Jo for doing so, reminding them that Mum had died of cancer. Dad, of course failed to notice, even when

I lit up in front of him. A year or two later he saw me with a cigarette in my hand and exclaimed in surprise, 'Oh, Tara, I didn't know you smoked.'

I started raiding the drinks cabinet with my friends because I knew Dad wouldn't notice. One night, after downing everything we could find, the scene in our bathroom resembled a hospital ward: one friend hanging over the toilet bowl, one over the sink, and one in the bath. I was the only one still standing. Even after a bottle of vodka, I never let go entirely, always maintaining a sense of responsibility, no matter how inebriated.

After all, who else was going to look after Dad? I had to teach him how to do the simplest of things. Everyday activities such as washing, cleaning, housework and cooking presented him with a confusing challenge. The washing machine, which my mother had finally succumbed to having as her health had failed her, was especially baffling for my father. I wrote out, point by point, how to work it, starting:

> *Step 1: Separate coloured clothes from white clothes.*
> *Step 2: Place clothes in machine.*
> *Step 3: Close door firmly.*
> *Step 4: Open tray and put one scoop of powder in left side.*

And so on. Except my father analysed every step, studying it for its intricacies, stopping to give his opinion on how the manufacturer might be able to improve the appliance. Three hours later, he still hadn't reached the eighth step, where the wash actually started. *I'm beginning to understand how you felt, Mum ...*

Sometimes, if I was really stuck, I would make the error of asking Dad to help me with my homework. He would reply with an hour-long monologue which went into every conceivable theory behind the concept in question. By the end I was so confused that I had no idea what the question meant. I had thought it was merely a 'yes' or 'no' answer – how silly of me.

Dad was always so engrossed in all the information that passed through his brain that you could walk right past him in the street and he wouldn't notice. On one occasion, when a friend rang and asked to speak with me, Dad told her that I had gone away for a few weeks. When I walked in the next morning, after a weekend away, he looked only mildly baffled to see me. Similarly our neighbours laughingly reported watching Dad walking down our street in London carrying a bag of wood for the fire. A stray log had fallen through a hole in the bottom of the bag. Upon realizing this, my father had diligently turned on his heel to pick it up, placing it carefully in the top of the bag. He had then continued on his way until another log fell through the same hole. Once more, upon noticing he had mislaid another piece of wood, my father had turned, stooped to pick it up and placed it patiently in the top of the bag. He continued in this manner all the way along the road, dropping log after log, much to our neighbours' amusement. It never occurred to him to actually fix the hole in the bottom of the bag.

You see, my father is unique, one of life's curious mysteries. He lives in another world, where seemingly superfluous information, such as where your daughter is or how a washing machine works, is discarded so as not to take up valuable brain space that could otherwise be used for more vital information, such as how neural pain pathways in the brain might react to opiates, or how India might solve its socio-economic problems. It was as if Dad's brain was locked on to an intellectual setting, where every task must be learned and analysed, as if he were studying for a university exam.

Meanwhile, all I wanted was to be 'normal'. I didn't feel as if I belonged. I tried my best to wear the 'right' clothes, which in London in the mid-eighties was ripped, faded, red-tab Levi 501 jeans, preferably at least two sizes too big, secured by a thick leather belt. It was especially cool if the legs were just a tad too long so that the ends would fray as they dragged along the ground.

One evening I decided I was going to go out with the trendy group from my school. I put on my very finest, most ripped pair of Levi 501s and doused myself in Anaïs Anaïs. I even put on make-up, agonizing for hours in front of the mirror as to how one was supposed to do it, using one of my mum's old bright red lipsticks. A rookie error, given the polarity of our skin tones, hair and eye colour.

I felt pathologically awkward. I stood on the platform at Camden Town underground station, trying desperately to think of something cool to say or at least to adopt a trendy stance, whatever that was. Clearly acting wasn't my strong point. I heard a female voice emanate from fifty yards down the platform, the voice of the super-cool beautiful 'It girl'.

'Look at Tara ... she's the odd one out,' she sang out loudly, repeating it just in case someone had missed it.

I froze, paralysed by the accuracy of her bullet. Whatever semblance of self-confidence or self-esteem I had, disintegrated in an instant. I didn't feel I belonged and now everyone knew it and thought it too.

Only my brother understood how it was.

When I was with Adam I felt I belonged. He made me feel safe. I didn't feel awkward. We didn't talk a lot about our feelings, about our grief, but in the years after Mum's death we built a shared understanding.

CHAPTER 8

Adam was beautiful, with chocolate-brown skin, straight shiny hair and a chiselled jaw. He was tall and could almost be classed as skinny, were it not that his frame was clad in sinewy muscle. There was not an ounce of fat on his lithe body. He was blessed with a brilliant intellectual mind but he was also highly sensitive, a deep thinker with an ever-questioning mind. He was only nineteen when he wrote in his diary:

Why should I be thinking so introspectively? I seek only honesty with myself, and in this mood I feel almost as though I know of the things I might want from life, but cannot grasp hold of the definite. Just let the words pour from inside without entering the analysis of my brain. Maybe in the confusion I shed a greater light on myself. I am writing, yet I feel as if I am seeing what I produce from someone else's point of view which in turn changes what I write and how I think.

Although he was bright and talented, he was disarmingly unassuming. When he was picked, out of hundreds, to take part in an episode of a TV series called *Shades of Darkness*, he never mentioned it to us, not until it was about to start filming, and then only to explain why he'd be missing a few days of school. He was embarrassed about his talents, as if he felt he wasn't worthy of them. He was compassionate well beyond his years, always thoughtful and caring of others.

The last couple of days have been so very thoughtful. I have thought of passion and compassion and why we have curbed them in our words when we feel so strongly in our hearts. I think, if I were to speak as these words are written, how much truer they would be to my romantic feelings, and yet, as usual I shall not, as sense will dictate to me how incongruous they would be with an everyday existence.

As an eighteen-year-old, he spent his Christmas working for the homeless. He relentlessly questioned life and the essence of happiness, particularly during his travels in India.

Delhi itself is forever hustling and bustling, millions of people occupying themselves in one fashion or another. It's so strange to think of them. What on earth do they do? Where do they find enjoyment and happiness? Or is survival the most prominent of desires in their hearts? Why I should question these things I do not really know, for if I think of London one may easily reason with similar terms: millions of people working all day to gain money which they can then spend and supposedly, hence, enjoy themselves.

Humans are adapted to their circumstances by nature, thus there is an up and down – whether that range is at all relative to one's environment I don't know. It is easy to say yes, for hunger is no joy. Yet perhaps the enjoyment for such an individual at having a full belly is a greater satisfaction than the enjoyment I have at one evening at the pub.

Adam had a huge concern for social justice, which sat awkwardly with his privileged upbringing and private education. The three of us all went to different schools: I to a single-sex state school with a good reputation; Jo to the tough local mixed comprehensive; Adam to a well-respected private school. His godmother had offered to contribute to the fees, but still the question hung in the air: 'Why did Adam go to a private school when both my parents held socialist ideals?' I don't think that either my mother or father realized the implications of their decision, the effect it would have on Adam and Jo.

Jo got the raw end of the deal. She knew it and so did Adam. The result of Jo's resentment at this inequality in our education was that Adam felt guilty. He also felt an immense pressure to succeed.

Aunt Margaret often came down to London to check on us, and to resolve any conflict.

'Adam's stolen my tennis racket!'

'I didn't steal it, I just borrowed it.'

'He always gets everything. How come he goes to a private school?'

'I can't help that, Jo. That was Mum and Dad's decision,' Adam said quietly.

I hated to hear them argue.

I had hoped that our loss would bring our family together, that we would somehow unite in our shared pain so that I would have a family once more. Instead we fragmented in our own grief. Four individual entities of pain floating randomly about the atmosphere, sometimes out of control and at other times settling for a while, sometimes shrinking, sometimes growing, but never touching.

Adam adored Jo. We both did, idolizing her, craving closeness. He scribbled in his diary:

Dear, dear Joby. What can I say, but that I love her. I desperately want to write to her, but even now I know I would want so much to say the 'right' words that I would undoubtedly say the wrong ones. I love and respect her so much that to be honest I want to say, speak and think on the same 'relating' terms. I know this is wrong for I can only be myself but it is something that has built up in me over the years and is not easy to remove.

44

Adam once wrote us notes entitled 'the big little sister' and 'the little big sister'. I was the big little sister because I am tall, broad-shouldered and strong, as well as being the youngest. Jo is smaller, but big in every other respect: capable, efficient and strong-minded. Just like Mum. After Mum's death, it often felt as if a no-entry sign was plastered across Jo's chest. Adam strove for her acceptance:

> *It's horrible in a way because I have this reverence, almost fear of Jobes. Perhaps fear is the wrong word, more like intimidation. I wonder how I might convince her that although I may not be as socially 'adequate' as her I still am myself and capable of dealing with things in my own way. At times it is almost as if she is guarding against me embarrassing myself. It's almost sometimes that I feel Jo just doesn't like me, which is fair enough as I'm pretty sure I've got a good idea of what she sees. Oh fuck, I don't know, but I respect her and above all I love her, she's my big sis.*

I too felt that Jo was out of reach, emotionally distant. It is only now that I realize that she had to be that way in order to survive.

All Adam and I knew was that we craved what we no longer had: unconditional love and comfort. And, as our father was unavailable, we looked to Jo. Neither of us had any idea of the pressure we were unwittingly passing up the line: me to Adam, Adam to Jo. We only knew there was pain and there was emptiness, and neither of us wanted it.

Jo and Adam were opposites. Grief and loss served only to accentuate the differences in their personalities. We had all lost the same person, yet our perceptions of that loss and the way we experienced the emptiness differed greatly. I was envious of Jo for the relationship she had had with Mum. They had often shouted and argued but they were friends. I knew they had had a special bond. I wished I could have had that. I wished that I had known Mum as a person, not just as 'Mum'.

I wasn't aware of the burden of responsibility Jo felt after Mum died. She was in her final year of school, studying for her A-levels. She had wanted to take a year off to go travelling after her exams but she sacrificed it to be there for us. With no idea of the pressure she was under, I saw only my world and her absence, and I wanted her to fill the gap that Mum had left. Like Adam, I strived for her approval and her love.

I searched for a rock, anything stable to help me keep my head above water. It was as if the rocks were all covered in slippery moss, so that every time I placed my hand upon one, it found a way to rid itself of me, sending me back into the murky water, gasping for air. I kept looking desperately for a solid handhold or foothold, so that I could draw breath. I found Adam.

He was the loose rock upon which I tentatively placed my foot so that I could haul myself out of the water and begin to climb my mist-shrouded mountain. I clung to him, for when I looked below I saw the abyss. We didn't talk about Mum, we simply loved and cared for each other.

CHAPTER 9

Adam and I shared a unique bond. Only my brother understood. It was as if, floating in our individual spheres of grief, we each held on to a small branch, which connected us and prevented us floating entirely alone. I have one artwork at home, a picture called *The Art of Life*. It is a painting of two hot-air balloons, one side lit up by the sun, the other side dark. In each basket stands a person. Each is reaching out to the other. They do not touch, and the balloons are separate, but there is a cord that runs between the two. Adam and me.

One day, Adam came home limping. I asked him what had happened.

'I hurt my foot,' he said, without looking at me.

'Yeah, I can see that, but how did you hurt it?'

I could tell he was embarrassed.

'I sort of ... kicked a door.'

I burst out laughing. 'Always good to pick a fight with a door.'

He smiled.

I found out later what had happened. Dad had left his keys at the cinema. Adam had told him to go back and find them. Dad had said he didn't want to walk back up the road, he'd get the locks changed instead. That was it. The point when Adam's frustration boiled over and he'd kicked the door. It was only a

47

small thing yet it signified so much more. It was a sign that all the turbulence and anger in my brother was metastasizing.

I loved to be around Adam. Most of the time he let me join in, though sometimes I managed to wind him up.

One Saturday morning I came and sat on the couch beside him while he watched the sport.

'Ad, I'm bored ...'

'Go read a book.'

'Talk to me ...'

'I'm watching football.'

I nudged him for a reaction, only I missed, and hit him where it hurt.

'Fuck, Tara!' His face was screwed up in pain. 'Why do you always spoil it?' But even as he said it I knew he was joking. He loved me as much as I loved him.

His favourite party trick was to get me to arm-wrestle his friends. He took great pleasure in watching his little sister beat them all. He always had time for me, always made me feel special. Adam had an incredible ability to do that for people.

If I was bullied, he would step in. If one of his friends fancied me, he would warn him off. We were proud of each other, protective.

Adam was the golden boy of our neighbourhood. As well as being smart, he was agile and strong, and good at rugby and cricket. I loved to watch him run up our street, ducking and diving, throwing dummies to each tree.

Boys wanted to be like him. Girls wanted to be with him, and they would stand at the top of the hill every morning, waiting to see Adam cycle past, giggling and flirting with him, much to his embarrassment.

I started going to the pub with my brother. I became 'someone': an avenue for girls to get to him. Adam was engaging and funny, with a quirky sense of humour but, although everyone liked to hang out with him, he felt the falseness of the Hampstead social scene, as did I. While Adam was a part of it because of the school he went to and because he was beautiful, he never felt at ease with it. He had an earthy genuineness about him which sat uncomfortably with the air kisses and affectedness of those around him. Like me, he struggled to belong:

Okay, so let's see. I like to buy the clothes that I have on tonight because I see myself in a particular image. Now, is it because I, myself, like these clothes or is it because other people will see me in a particular way, which is not necessarily what I am? Can I answer? I suppose it must be the second because that is the one I would least like to admit to.

It was no surprise when Adam was made head boy at his school, and even less of a surprise that he never told us. He was a straight-A student, gifted in everything he did, but his drive and perfectionism came at a cost. The letter my mother had written to him before she died added to my brother's burden, something she couldn't have foreseen when she wrote it.

My dear Adam,
I don't know when you will read this, but you are fifteen as I write it. I am very proud of you and love you dearly and want you to know that. You will have most of your life still before you and it makes me very sad to realize I have shared so little of it with you. I presume you will miss me, but once all of you have recovered from your sadness I hope you will pick up the threads of your lives again, piece them together in a meaningful way and gradually, when the grieving is over, the happy memories will sustain you.
*   You have a special place in my life, Adam. A mother's only son inevitably makes her proud and full of expectation and hope. We have tried as you know to give you the sort of education that we thought you could benefit from, but it has been difficult for me as you know I have a socialist philosophy and do not believe in an elitist society. On the other hand, I do believe that a chap's*

potential should be encouraged and developed to the full and you have plenty of that. Diligence and single-mindedness and a sense of direction will, I am sure, achieve for you a university place. I'm sure that is your aim as well as Dad's and mine and of course whatever you do afterwards is up to you. I have always nursed a dream that my son should go to Oxbridge, specifically, I think, because it is something in the family that nobody has yet achieved. Maybe you will be the first to do so! But wherever you go, enjoy your university days – alas Dad will find it hard financially but you will get a grant and you will simply have to live on it, but then lots of chaps do.

Always in life, the more you put into it the more you will get out of it, and always remember that whatever you do, you are part of the community, the wider world, and every citizen has a responsibility toward that community, to care, to give and to take a share in responsibility for it.

You will, I am sure, be able to help Dad a lot – he will need it. Jo will be able to cope herself, but Tara will need all of you. Do help each other all you can and try to see each other's needs. I have trusted Jo through her adolescence and I trust you too. Above all, Adam, be happy and fulfilled.

Goodbye my son and good luck.

All my love

Mum

Adam read these words often, and he held them close to him, just as I did mine. The message was clear: he must fulfil his mother's expectations; he must go to Oxford; he must be responsible and give to the community; he must help Dad and look after his sister. Mum had unwittingly passed a poisoned chalice to her son, full of her own hopes and dreams. She had written the letter in good faith, pouring out the love of a mother for her son, striving to give a lifetime of guidance in those few lines. But she had also planted a seed of unimaginable pressure, which Adam carried: a constant, heavy load upon his young shoulders. The words were expressed in one instant of one day in my mother's life, yet for my brother they coloured his whole life. Adam took those words and chose them to guide him through the confusion of adolescence, his search for identity and his place in the world.

CHAPTER 10

I walked into Adam's room at home. I took in the array of papers, books and empty coffee cups strewn across the desk. He had just taken the Oxford entrance exam.

'How was it, Ad?'

He shrugged. 'Bloody hard. I think I stuffed it.'

'You didn't want to go there anyway. You'll have much more fun if you go to Edinburgh.'

He looked angry with himself.

I should have known better. Adam was granted a place at Balliol College, Oxford, to study chemistry, just as Mum and Dad had hoped. He remained indifferent, humble in his achievements, unsure of his direction.

He took a gap year before starting university, travelling first to France to learn French, and later to India. I missed my big bro terribly. I was still at school, studying for my A-levels. It was just Dad and me in the house now. Mother's Day was always tough but this year particularly so. I felt empty and alone, wishing Ad was there. He was in Grenoble, in France. He had just finished reading *Sons and Lovers* by DH Lawrence. In his diary he scribbled a quote from the book.

Mother's Day, 1988

For me ...

'They could not establish between themselves and an outsider just the ordinary human feeling and unexaggerated friendship; they were always restless for something deeper. Ordinary folk seemed shallow to them, trivial and inconsiderable. And so they were unaccustomed, painfully uncouth in the simplest social intercourse, suffering and yet insolent in their superiority. Then beneath was the yearning for soul-intimacy to which they could not attain because they were too dumb, and every approach to close connection was blocked by their clumsy contempt of other people. They wanted genuine intimacy, but they could not get even normally near to anyone, because they scorned to take the first steps, they scorned the triviality which forms common human intercourse.'

Just as I did, on Mother's Day Adam yearned more than ever for intimacy, for connection, for something deeper. He read voraciously, seeking in books an expression of those things he found difficult to describe himself:

Oh God, how I wish that my reality was in the stories I read. Again, understandably so, as Dostoyevsky says. Is not their reality a truer one? Are we not merely their diluted forms? Unable to speak the feelings they pronunciate.

In books Adam found a tenuous link to his own reality, a reality that he could not express to the world. I didn't feel I belonged. Neither did my brother. He scorned himself for his inability to connect with those around him. For me, I found that connection in him.

He came home from France and for a few happy months I had my bro back as he saved money to travel to India, took his little sister out to the pub and explained electrode potentials to her on an almost daily basis. In July he travelled to India with his best friend Dan and his journal.

I missed him terribly. The house felt empty without him, but he sent postcards and letters full of his quirky humour, addressing mine to 'the big little one'.

My dear, dear little sister,
I don't actually see why I should be writing to you as I believe I have never received any correspondence from you in the whole of my life, have I, Snoobie? Wait ... Actually somewhere from the depths of my memory I do remember a 'Hi, having a great time. Love Ta.' Hmmm ... Yes, well, I hope this letter can be equally ... precise! Anyway, Plopper, I hope that Greece was not too outrageous and that nothing of any improper nature occurred, ie the partaking of alcohol, drugs and men, and that the cultural experience was fully appreciated, this of course being the purpose of the visit. That leaves me with just one last thing to say Teej. Err ... you know the 16th of September, very ordinary sort of a day, sort of a nice day ... Err, my birthday (I didn't think you'd forget). Well, seeing as I'll be on a bloody Indian train to Delhi, I thought it might be nice if on the 18th when I get back, I might have a nice meal waiting for me or something like that – wouldn't that be nice, eh Ta? Yeh, I thought you'd like the idea. Shit, no space. Anyway, see you then.
Love Big Bro

I laughed. I didn't see that he was reaching out to me. There had been one occasion, when Mum was ill, when we had all forgotten Adam's birthday. About halfway through the day he'd quietly reminded us. 'I'm getting to be a big boy now,' he'd said. My mother was guilt-stricken and horrified. Since then it had always been a family joke. I scribbled an equally light-hearted note back:

I might possibly manage to have dinner waiting for you when you get back if you're very nice ...

I smiled, teasingly. He didn't sound unhappy. He scrawled in his diary:

Soon I will be twenty. My teenage years will have merged into the past, but in essence I will be the same. As always a birthday indicates no change in the individual, but merely what is expected of him or her by others. To me, twenty is old. It sounds like an age of maturity, but, God, how young I feel to fill its shoes. Well, time passes and, as Nehru says, the present is a culmination of the past and future and all three states we must experience as flowing into the other in order to appreciate life to its full. So, really, age is a nonsensical concept for it only describes the one tense of present.

Adam had been to India the previous summer on a school trip trekking in the Himalayas. I knew how much India fascinated him, how free he was of the pressure he felt in London. Yet this year was different. Gone was the carefree fascination, replaced with an intense dark shroud:

I am still feeling that great vacant misery that I left with, and what it is due to, I don't fully understand. All life everywhere in the world suddenly seems small and insignificant, a place where everything is strange and somehow pathetically sad. One could die here and nobody would notice. God, I want some company. I want to see Jo and Ta, and Dad, sweet little Daddy.

While I cried, Adam wrote, and read, and kicked the occasional door. India triggered his analytical mind. At nineteen years old he questioned life relentlessly, haunted by his mother's dying wishes.

I see that your life is as you yourself mould it, but in a way it makes me fearful. I question: can I really be that individual? Can I really

55

do what I am capable of? Am I worthy of the opportunities I have? Here in India, all around me I see enthusiasts. People following what they want, not questioning and so confusing their own minds with doubts as to whether they might achieve or be considered to have achieved what they intended. Theirs is a love of life for life's sake itself.

Anyway, I know myself what I should do. I must throw off this doubt and find the courage to make attempts at things, no matter the results. I am not a courageous man, but so long as I am aware of this, then hopefully I shall make myself one. Not a natural courage, but through practice maybe it shall become so. Step forth into the world. I owe so many people, I cannot fail them.

Adam thought he should be perfect. That was what the world expected and what his mother expected. Anything less was not good enough. Although he was travelling with Dan, he didn't divulge his anguish to him. Only in his writing did he do that as he struggled to make sense of the world.

Whenever words strike me at the heart, I myself am struck by a weeping sadness. I see through a crystal window how vapid my efforts at describing living and wearing life have been. Any fated moments of elucidation have been bent by the concourse of time, twisted and lost in the numbing canals of memory.

To have painted truth in words that are the very shadows of my soul, to write, to imagine and to be …

No one knew of his inner turmoil. He kept it hidden. People on the outside saw only the vibrant, caring, compassionate Adam, the boy who halted his own ascent of a mountain on a school trip in the Himalayas to go back and render assistance to his teacher, helping him to conquer the summit that had defeated him in previous years; the boy who steadfastly cared for his sister and his friends. This was the Adam that those close to him saw.

Only his writing betrayed the dichotomy between the face he showed to the world and the conflicted, questioning, internal

Adam. He searched relentlessly ... for understanding, for purity, for clarity.

I feel at the moment – the draining in the stomach as if my natural humanness is filtering away. Please pray that I do not, once more, become the sterile alien. God, I want to be furious, but this half-baked, half-there, half-worried, half-relaxed mind and heart of mine will not let pure feeling through.

He arrived home from India just a few days after his twentieth birthday. I had missed him dreadfully and was counting the days until his return.

When he walked in, I was shocked. It wasn't only the traditional Indian clothes he was wearing that made him look a stranger: his face looked hollow-eyed and ashen. My bubble of excitement burst instantly, giving way to a frightening sense of impending doom.

'How come you're so late?'

'I got searched at the airport. They found a pipe in my bag so they strip-searched me. They read my diaries.'

'Ad, you're shaking,' I said, confused and worried.

His face was vacant, as if he wasn't there. The person in front of me didn't feel like my brother.

'I'm just excited to be home,' he said, but his voice and body language belied his words.

I stood there waiting for him to say something else. When he did, he spoke in a monotone: 'I was walking down the street and this little old lady passed me. She said, "Don't like the likes of you around here."'

I was indignant. 'Oh Ad, you should have told her you were about to go to Oxford and that you were the head boy at University College School. Then see what she had to say!'

I was burning up with fury. *How dare she? Didn't she know he was perfect?*

The only thing that shone from his ghostly face was utter devastation. I stood and watched his spirit dissolve before my eyes. I wanted him to be Ad again, my normal, funny, big brother. I wanted to reach out and touch him and bring him back from whatever awful distant place he was in, but it was as if he was behind a panel of shatterproof glass through which I couldn't reach. He looked at me. No flicker of life in his eyes.

'We bought you a bike for your birthday so you can cycle around Oxford.'

'Thanks,' he said, without enthusiasm.

All I knew at the time was that he looked and felt absolutely disconnected from me, and from the world.

CHAPTER 11

Two weeks later, Adam started his degree at Balliol, scrawling a letter to me before he left, leaving it on the kitchen table:

Dear TJ
Take good care of yourself. I'm going to miss you lots. And baby, even if things look really bad, remember, all of us, Jo, Dad and I, will always be here. If you ever want to talk, just write to me. I will write anyway as no doubt I'm going to feel quite lonely at first as well.
All my love Ad xxx

PS We are all individuals and however incapable we may seem to ourselves we all manage in the end.

Adam had never wanted to go to Oxford. The elitism didn't sit comfortably with him. I had tried to persuade him that he could choose a different university, that he didn't have to follow the path Mum and Dad had laid out for him, but he saw going to Oxford as his duty.

India had only heightened Adam's discomfort. Having immersed himself in the suffering and hardship of life there, he felt the inequality even more acutely. He could not reconcile his fortunate life, with advantages handed to him on a plate, with the millions of poverty-stricken lives in India.

When we were sitting in the railway restaurant there was a man, an Untouchable, sweeping the floor. Down on all fours as dirty as the ground he was cleaning. God, it made me angry. This human being, this 'child of God', subjected to such an eternity. How weak and defenceless had society made him, how accepting of his fate. Thoughts like 'stand up, be a man' pounced on my brain, but they weren't my thoughts ... just memories of some film-inspired clichés. But, oh God, how full was my heart with sadness, how I wanted to do the right owed to him ... how disgusting is human nature. I wanted to stand up and – in that oh-so-hackneyed way – pull him to his feet and shout to everyone, 'This is a man, not a mongrel.' Oh fuck it, it's a load of bollocks but it was the truth. Obligingly, I have written it as it was thought, as tacky and vulgar as it sounded to myself. And, oh how so very patronizing. Great saint gives beggar pride ... God, unthinkingly base of me – shit, shut up.

Adam's world was in conflict with his conscience. How could he go to Balliol while billions of people starved in the world? He could find no justice in what he saw, no comfortable terrain on which to stand. Even the charity work he did for the homeless did little to assuage his feelings of guilt.

I was seventeen and in my final year of school. A-levels loomed. I was about to take part in a selection weekend for Operation Raleigh, a charity for young people to experience community work and adventure projects in developing countries. An ex-participant had come to give a talk at school about his experiences and it had immediately grabbed my attention.

Adam had given me an SAS survival guidebook to help me. I read the book from cover to cover in my desperation to be selected.

After the weekend, I couldn't wait to tell Adam how it had gone.

Monday 10 October 1988

Dear little Addie,
How's it going? I want to hear all about it so I expect a letter in
return. You never know, you might even get a visit from your little
sis (or should I say big sis?).

I've just had the toughest weekend of my life, but also one of
the best. I went on the Operation Raleigh selection weekend. It was
absolutely brilliant! We had to run everywhere in our groups with
packs and all to different grid/map references, where we had to pick
up various things – inner tubes, poles, paddles and a plastic bag
containing a rabbit (our dinner!) which I later had to skin, cook on
a fire and eat! In fact it didn't taste too bad at all – just like chicken.
Mind you, anything would taste good at ten o'clock at night having
run around all day! We had to solve all these problems like how to
get over an eight-foot high electric fence with three poles and some
rope, and how to get across this river with ten planks and fourteen
empty plastic containers. Then we had to make a raft out of the
inner tubes and poles. One of the best things about it was being in
the team. Everyone really encouraged and helped each other. By the
end I really felt close to them.

It was brilliant to get away and not even think about work
for two days. It was just what I needed, although it did make me
wonder why I'm sitting in school when I could be out there doing
something like that, but I guess it has to be done! Anyway, Addie,
I'm knackered now (despite having slept fourteen hours last night,
trying to recover!) so I'll say goodnight!
Lots & lots & lots & lots & lots & lots of love and kisses and hugs
TJ

Monday 17 October 1988

Dear Addie – I've just received a letter of congratulations from
Operation Raleigh saying that I've been selected to go on an
expedition – wicked, eh? I can't wait. Mind you, I have to raise

61

£2,200! Just a minor problem! They haven't told me much about the expeditions yet except that there are two to Australia, two to Zimbabwe and one to Chile, and I have to put down a list of three in order of preference.

So ... Addie, how are you? I hope you're working hard. Have you done anything about changing courses yet? Get yourself together and do something about it, okay? That's an order, by the way!

I'm not really a nagging little sister, am I? But, Addie, I hope you are looking after yourself and are happy. You just have to make a big, big effort. Ultimately it's only you that can make yourself happy. You can't rely on other people. I know it sounds ridiculous, but I really have found that if you smile more, just when you're walking down the street or sitting in your room and thinking – it really does make you feel much happier. So stop dwelling on everything you think you should be, but aren't, and don't think about things so much – just get up and do them! I know it's hard and I don't practise what I preach, but please try.

Anyway, end of lecture number 500,000. Wake up, Adam, don't worry, I've finished. I'd better go because it's time for Neighbours! Lots and lots of hugs.

Love

TJ xxx

CHAPTER 12

Adam sat, desolate at his desk in Room 36, Staircase 22, Balliol College, Oxford, one of the most prestigious learning institutions in the world. Images of India kept flashing though his mind, and especially the Untouchable on his hands and knees cleaning the floor. He stared out of his window to the quad below. Masters in academic gowns strolled confidently across the perfectly mown grass. Didn't anyone else feel the inequality? Where was the compassion? What was the point? An overwhelming emptiness seemed to be encroaching relentlessly on his very being.

He stared at the chemistry essay in front of him. The wall next to his desk was lined with empty Marlboro packets.

Adam's mind raced, flipping between meaningless trivia, the injustice in the world, and the chemistry essay that sat before him. *Fuck it, why bother. I don't want to do this, anyway.* Then suddenly there was India again, and the Untouchable at the station. Why hadn't he helped him? He was just as useless as the master walking across the quad. He couldn't get control of his head. Only alcohol seemed to numb the confusion and to temper the flashes of frightening darkness that appeared within him like a devil poised to strike. He took out a piece of paper and started writing to his sister.

17 October 1988

Dear TJ,

Glad to hear the weekend went well, not surprising really, what with your SAS guidebook to survival. Well, I'm pretty pissed at the moment, but I'll try to phrase a letter of some sort. Mind you, I've got a right to be as I've just finished a twenty-page essay on some fucking chemistry crap. I can't fucking believe how much work I've done so far. Two nights in a row I've been up until four thirty in the morning, not having a laugh but instead trying to write this bloody essay. They don't half ask for work. Anyway, enough about boring shitty work – what about the people? Well, there are good people here; it's just that I'm not really in the mood to get to know them. I don't really know how to do that anyway (which is probably nearer the truth). It's so bloody hard to accustom oneself to the idea that this is what one has chosen to do. Don't get me wrong, Booga, it's not that the place is getting me down, it's only myself. You know how it is: when you're not thinking, you have a laugh, and as soon as you do, you wonder why on earth?

I've talked to the dean about changing course, by the way; he is a bit of a big boss, but politics, philosophy and economics doesn't seem possible unless I do the whole of the first-year chemistry. The worst thing is, I don't really know quite how much I'm interested in doing it anyway. Dilemmas. Anyway, I'm going to see him tomorrow to make a decision. Fuck, I might end up giving the whole place a holy piss off and doing English A-level. Shit, it's so hard to judge. The old emotions are going up and down like a yo-yo. One minute I feel as if I can cope with everything, the next I'm quiet and don't say a word to anyone. No basis for making friends, really. Oh well, life rolls on. Shit, it's almost 1am. Gotta get some sleep. But before I do, Taj, thanks for writing.

However much truth seems weird, it's all we can do to obey it. Heavy concept to stimulate the Joji vibes. By the way, send my love to her and to Dad. Maybe he might even like to write to me?

And you, Teej, come up if you want to, we'll go for a piss up. Until then, little sis, take care and don't let the work get you down.

Keep smiling.
Love Ad xxx

Monday 7 November 1988

Dear Addie,
You old codger ... How's it going? Keeping up with the old fitness regime I hope! Daniel, the old slapper, has insisted that I go to the Arsenal versus Liverpool match on Wednesday – oh dear! I told him I was going to wear a Tottenham scarf, but he said I'd get mashed, so I went off the idea pretty rapido!

I have just spent three hours (almost!) hoovering the whole of the house, including your and Jo's rooms, so it is now spic and span! Well, maybe that's a slight exaggeration, but it does look better.

Dad has finally unblocked his ears – not that it makes any difference when you try to speak to him! By the way I spoke to big Joji yesterday. She kept asking when we were going to go up and see her. So how about the weekend of the 26th/27th November? I'll have done my Oxford entrance exam by then and it's the week before you break up. Anyway, standard electrode potentials are calling so I'd better go!
Love you lots and lots and lots.
Big hugs and kisses.
TJ xxx

PS Take care, my little moojie ... and whenever you feel completely pissed off with everything ... I'm always here, feeling just as lonely as you.

London, 14 November 1988

Dad, as usual, had his nose buried in a book in the living room. He was present but for all intents and purposes, he was absent. I sat at our kitchen table talking to Ben, my sister's ex-boyfriend. Talking and crying. It was Monday and Adam had been down at the weekend. He'd had that pale, strained, blank look about him. We had gone for a run together. He had talked about trying to change courses, about not knowing what he wanted or what was wrong with him. He spoke about quitting Oxford, about feeling down.

I'd never seen him like that. He saw nothing good in himself, was consumed with the idea that he wasn't as good as everyone thought he was. I did my best: I told him to exercise, to run, and to leave Oxford. He could have the rest of the year off and then go to Edinburgh. He kept telling me it was okay, not to worry, he'd sort it. Yet I wasn't so sure about that: he was a skeleton without a spirit, a faint shadow of the Adam I knew.

I was relieved that Ben was there, and that I could share my worries. We were close; he had been there through my mother's death.

'I've never seen him like that. He looked terrible.'

'Ta, just worry about yourself. Look after yourself. Adam will be okay.'

'I'm scared; I don't know what to do.'

'He'll be okay, Ta. He really will.'

I went to bed with puffy eyes. *He'll be okay*, I kept saying to myself. *Keep writing, phoning.* But I'd had that feeling of foreboding before. It was uncomfortably familiar.

Balliol College, Oxford, November 1988 (not dated)

Dearest little Teej,

Thanks for the letter. By now you'll have seen the footy match, which I hope, went the way of the correct team – that's Liverpool, of course, despite what Dan may say. Has he inspired you as much as Dan's songs inspired me in India? You know, the sort of highly prophetic and artistic yodelling of 'come on you gooners' and 'you're going home in a red and white ambulance'. Yes, I thought as much. He had such a lovely habit of crying out such poetic lines in the most appropriate places, e.g., Hindu temples, Muslim temples, Sikh temples and every other place of religious sanctitude. I think it's all part of his acute cultural sensitivity myself. By the way, send the little gooner my regards and of course tell him he's a cunt.

As for everything else. Well, it's going along. Ta, don't worry. I'll sort it. Not quite sure how as I'm getting myself further and further into a mess. I made the application to change courses to human sciences, but it's not as simple as that. I have to apply to a separate committee and have an interview. And really I don't want to do it anyway and ... I'm going mad ...
Goodbye
Love your ...?

Panic, his mind swirling, colours spinning ... Breathe, try again, stay calm ... What is happening? ... What is happening?

London, 21 November 1988
Oxford Entrance Exam, Paper 1, General Paper

I walked into the examination room. Why was I here? I didn't want to go to Oxford. I wasn't smart enough anyway. I knew that. I thought of Adam and how miserable he was and recalled his last letter to me.

Dear Teej,
Your Oxford entrance exams must be pretty soon so I thought I'd send you a quick note to wish you luck. Hope the whole business hasn't stressed you out too much, and anyway, you're doing it only for yourself. So, if you don't really want to come here, it doesn't matter in any case. Hope Dad hasn't been applying too much emotional pressure. I know it's hard, but just do what you want in the end. Dad won't expect anything else ...

I stared at the exam question. *Can someone else be a better judge of my interests than I am myself?* It was an open question, to be interpreted freely, allowing a special few to shine: those blessed with supreme intelligence. I had nothing brilliant or unique to write. My brain kept veering back to Adam.

I started to scribble things down, trying to answer the question but I found myself writing, on and on, about Adam: how he couldn't see the beautiful person that he was; how twisted his view of himself was compared with what the world saw; how he couldn't see his talents, only his faults. Did I answer the question on the exam paper? Maybe, vaguely, but I didn't care; I had written what was in my heart.

I got up and left, knowing I had failed.

Balliol College, Oxford, 21 November 1988

Adam sat in his room. Flat, empty, disconnected. The words flowed from his pen:

I want to write a final statement of what I am. I am weak-willed, lazy, insecure and very stupid. I wasn't once, that's true. However, I have been living by that fact for a number of years now. Everybody believes it isn't true, but unfortunately it is. All life is passing me by now. The only way I see it in some part of its fire is unfortunately when I am drunk, when not worried by anything in the world. The rest of the time it is a chore, a dream waiting to end. The only reason for this is because I have made it so, by convincing myself that this is what it is like. But these words do actually have meaning.

Unfortunately I also realize that I cannot live like this because there are so many people that love me in all honesty. I cannot match their love and so I cannot allow myself to destroy them as I have destroyed myself. My whole life has been a catharsis – look at my 'writings'.

You will all explain the reasons wrongly. I'll tell you why, because I have lied all my life. I have cried all my life, because I wasn't perfect and I couldn't accept it.

London, 21 November 1988, 8.30pm

It was my best friend Jess's eighteenth birthday. We were walking on Hampstead Heath with her boyfriend Dan, Adam's best friend. Jess had also sat the Oxford entrance exam that day; only, unlike me, she wanted to get in.

Dan and Ad had travelled India together and seen each other through some rocky times. Like Adam, Dan hadn't fitted the mould of the private school they had attended. They shared the sense of wanting to discover more about the world, about life, and they both knew what it was to struggle. Adam loved him.

The three of us talked about Oxford, about why Jess wanted it so much and why I didn't. I told them what I had written in the exam. We talked about Adam and wished that he was with us. We planned a visit to Oxford to see him the following weekend. We'd go for a piss-up and cheer him up.

I said goodbye to my friends and wandered back along the road toward home. I opened the door. All was quiet and dark. I walked slowly up the stairs to my mattress on the floor (because that was the cool way to have it). I closed my eyes and slept.

Balliol College, 22 November 1988, 1.30am

Dear Teej,
Cheers for the letter. Don't know what is happening, can't even write any more. Want to die now. Well, I don't really but at least it might give me something of a solid decision …

Fear … mind racing … chemistry equations, images battering from every direction. Confusion, panic … no way out … no way out … scrawling things on paper …what's happening … what's happening …?

To my dear family,

What I have done is because ….

All I want to say to all my family is that I love them more than I could ever love anybody. My mind is hardly functioning so if I can just relate the last vestiges of humanity that remain within me, let me do so.

To Ta, I have done this because I am selfish. If I hadn't, I would remain this soft negative sponge that I have been over the past year. Ta, just think that this is what I wanted to do. Give me that. I have few feelings left. This is one of them.

To Jo, all my admiration and love. You are a person I wish I could have been.

To Dad, I'm sorry, Father; I didn't have the guts to stay with it.

To Mags, how could I have let everyone down?

You all thought I am something which I am not. I hope you will forgive me. I just couldn't be bothered any more, because I cannot be bothered with anything.

NOTHING I HAVE EVER DONE ...

I want to be with Mum ...

The window ... open it ... climb through it ... over ... head-first ... end the pain ...

Black.

CHAPTER 13

The phone ringing intruded into my dreams. I stirred, vaguely wondering who could be calling at this time. Then I heard the familiar trudge of my dad's heavy footsteps as he climbed the stairs. He knocked on my bedroom door. I glanced at the clock. It was 2.16am.

'Uh … uh …Tara,' he spoke through the doorway.

'Yes, Dad, what is it? Who was on the phone?'

'It's Adam … He's had an accident.' His voice stuttered; the words came in disjointed pieces. 'He's in hospital … I … I … ha—have to go to Oxford.'

He wasn't making sense.

My body froze. 'What do you mean, he's had an accident? Is he okay?'

'I don't know … I have to go.'

'Can I come?'

'No, stay here … This had better not be some bloody hoax.'

I heard the anger in his voice.

That's how it was: the instant that changed my life forever. There is a reason they call it the dead of night. Four years earlier I had been thirteen when I had woken in the middle of the night needing to say goodbye to my mother. Now I was seventeen and it was Adam.

Nobody knew what had happened: Dad didn't, nor did the police. I knew, though. My body was screaming the truth at me, great waves of repulsion sweeping through it. And, as hard as my body screamed, my head fought against what was utterly inconceivable.

I lay in bed, my body convulsed with fear while my mind went through different scenarios endlessly.

2.30am: *Had he had a car accident?*
3am: Overwhelming fear. *Nothing could happen to him.*
3.30am: Panic. *I should be with him.*
4am: *Maybe he's okay?*
4.30am: *What's happening?*
5am: Crushing, frightening loneliness.
5.30am: *Please, God. Let this night end.*
6am: All-consuming dread enveloping every cell in my body.
6.30am: Morning at last, and a phone call from a neighbour.

'Adam's in hospital. Your dad's there.'
'I want to go. I want to be with Adam.'
'No, Tara. Dad wants you to go to school, take the exam. Wait for your sister to get here.'
I want to be with Adam. Why won't anyone let me get to him?
I could see his face. He needed me. Even if he was unconscious, he'd know I was there. He'd wake up for me. I knew he would. I could not bear the thought that he would wake and I would not be there.
Go to school to sit the second Oxford exam ... ironic, impossible, ridiculous. Were they all mad? Someone, please let me get to Oxford ...
I went to school. I didn't take the exam. I waited for Jo. *Please hurry ...*

That afternoon, Jo drove us to Oxford. All we knew was that Adam had 'fallen' from his window and hit his head.
Please get there. Please get there ... Lost ... Which way to the Radcliffe Infirmary? The intensive care unit ... A nurse explaining:

72

'Adam is on life support. There are tubes attached to him to help him breathe. You can talk to him. He might be able to hear you.'

I walked into the room. Adam's words flashed before me: *There before me lay the scaffold of my soul, the support upon which my own life had grown.* I sat with Adam, holding his hand. It was limp and cold. His eyes were swollen, oozing, eerily open just a slit, glistening. Were they tears? Tubes pulled at the side of his mouth. I watched as his body jerked and the monitors made a beeping sound, lines zig-zagging up and down on a screen.

He's choking. Do something. Help him.

'Just a cough,' the nurse explained when she saw the panic in my face.

I wanted to be alone with Adam. Just me and him. Only I understood. Only me and my brother. *Go away, everyone. Leave me alone with my brother.*

Then, at last, a little time alone with him.

'It's okay, Ad, I understand,' I whispered. I needed him to know that it was okay, he was not alone, and I forgave him.

I laid my head on his hand, just wanting to be close, just me and my brother touching each other's souls. At last some time, a stolen moment, just me and him ...

'Are you okay?' The voice of my dad's well-meaning friend sliced murderously between Adam and me, robbing me of my one last moment of connectedness with my beautiful sacred brother.

'Piss off!' I wanted to yell. 'Fuck off! You don't belong here.' But once again no sound came and I swallowed my anger and my resentment.

They told me that if Adam woke he might never be the same again. I said I knew, but I didn't. I didn't care: I just wanted him back at any cost. This couldn't happen. I couldn't lose him.

The days ticked by. I existed, somehow, surviving one second to the next. Friends arrived one by one as the news spread. I remember their faces, grey and strained. Then, one day, it might have been day three or four, or perhaps it was day six or seven, or eight, I don't know, I was sitting in the waiting area outside the intensive care unit with my aunt Margaret when the heaviness that I had carried with me since the night of the phone call began to morph into an immense crushing vice, clamped across my chest, strangling me. I could not breathe, I could not cry, I could not move. It was as if I was crammed into a one-foot-square transparent box that was slowly filling with water.

I couldn't do it, I couldn't survive, I needed a pill, and I needed it to go away, I was going mad.

Someone help me breathe. Please give me something, anything to take it away. Please put me to sleep ...

I went over to my aunt and knelt on the floor at her feet, my hands on her lap. 'I need help. I need them to give me something. I can't breathe.'

Then, as I said the words, a dam burst inside me, releasing an unstoppable tsunami of grief. Pulsating howls. Raw pain.

Just as words cannot adequately describe love, so they cannot adequately convey unimaginable pain.

In the years that followed, I would have many such tidal waves of emotion, but never one as hauntingly intense as that. I often wonder how it must have been for my aunt Margaret to live that moment with me, while she was also immersed in her own grief. There have been few people in my life that have been able to take the weight of such emotion. My aunt was the first, and it bound me to her. Without her, I do not believe I would have survived. She shared my pain then, as she does to this day.

I wanted to see Adam's room as he had left it. I needed to understand. Then Jo told me that she had gone to Adam's room in Balliol in the middle of the night. She had moved things and cleared his desk. I was furious. Perhaps she'd had a moment in the darkness where she'd needed to say goodbye, as I had with Mum, but I didn't care. What about me? What about what I needed? Why hadn't she asked me?

How could I say goodbye, how could I understand, if I couldn't see Adam's room as he'd left it? He would have left me a clue. I knew he would. He would have left something for me, something I could hold on to. I needed to be able to piece together his final moments. Jo had taken that from me.

Adam was mine, not hers. I was closest to him. She had hurt him. He didn't want her, he wanted me.

I wanted to lash out, to scream and shout, but I didn't. I never voiced my anger or my needs.

Dad was adamant that someone had to be held accountable. Someone had done this to Adam.

They did an electro-encephalogram of my brother's brain. There was no sign of life. Only the tubes kept him breathing. Dad didn't believe the doctors; he thought they were corrupt.

'Do another one.' Nothing.

'And another one.'

He's gone, Dad, he's gone.

I understand why people in this position cannot comprehend that their beloved is dead. The machines lie, imitating life, allowing you to believe what you yearn to believe. Why would you choose to terminate that hope? Switching off the life support feels like driving a suicide bomb into your family home. I wanted to cling to my brother's beating heart, and so did my father.

The machine kept Adam breathing, kept his heart beating, for nine interminably long days, days that remain in my memory as a continuous dull gnawing emptiness interspersed by lightning strikes of terrifying clarity. I understand why doctors give sedatives to people in grief yet I am glad I didn't have any. I believe that I had to live through those days, feeling the pain, in order to start the healing. That way, I could begin a fragile and tenuous reconnection to life. I had to know absolutely and completely how it felt to be in the quicksand, beneath the earth at the very base of my mountain. Only then could I could begin my slow crawl out of it.

CHAPTER 14

After Adam died, Dad and I lived on in the house. It was a shell now, no longer a family home, and I hated it. I looked at photographs of the five of us and I could only see that half were gone. I thought of Adam's words:

As for myself, I am so terribly sad again. I wonder to myself what is there in this world that I can want, or desire to do. I flash pictures through my head of home, of places all over the world, and yet all seems bland and without interest. What is worse, is that it makes me quiet and resentful of everything around me.

Inside the house, Dad and I lived separately, individual bodies of pain. We never touched; we never shared our grief with one another. It was simply too painful.

My father never returned to the psychiatric hospital. He didn't, couldn't process the pain of it all. Full awareness would have killed him.

Much later, Dad told me that if it hadn't been for me and Jo, he would have slit his throat. In the years that followed the deaths of Mum and Adam, he lived out his pain in the cruellest of ways, full of anger, regret and blame. There is a quiet rage within him that I see when he talks of the past, of Mum and Adam. It is a passive anger, more powerful in many ways than any overt display of aggression.

A year after Adam's death my father moved to the country, to a house in the middle of nowhere. He gave Adam's life insurance money to charity. He gave his television and video to a taxi driver in lieu of payment for a ride. He shunned all his friends so that he could live alone with his pain.

I started having panic attacks, although initially I didn't know what they were. They would leap out at me unexpectedly, and it was as if a blanket had been thrown over my head. My heart raced, a cold sweat erupted from my skin. *What's happening? That's what Ad wrote ... Am I going mad? That's what Ad had said ... Dad's been in a psychiatric hospital, Adam killed himself. What if it's me next? What if I'm not normal? What if I scream? Then they'll think I'm mad. What if I go crazy?* One fear fuelled another until the terror consumed me. It was as if I had taken on all the anxieties and fears that Adam had borne.

I believe that Adam suffered similarly from panic attacks. In the months after his death, as I found myself living through so much of the same confusion and fear that he had written about in his final days, I thought I had an inkling of what he had gone through. He had probably thought about taking his own life many times, but it was panic that drove those final moments, before he climbed out of his window at Balliol. Adam had given us the answer when he wrote: *In sudden breaths of reality, the present engulfs me.* On 22 November 1988 at 1.30am the present moment finally swallowed him up.

Had it not been for Margaret I would not have survived. I went to Edinburgh and stayed in her home. I sat on her beanbag and we talked. She had lost her husband, my mother's brother, very suddenly, just two years before, but still she managed to be a rock for me, for all of us.

Margaret had been one of the very few who had recognized Adam's inner turmoil in the months before his death, and she had written to my father outlining her concerns. Ad always spoke fondly of her.

I just got a letter from Mags, which was cool; the old stomper is a great old dongo really. Using all her hip and trendy London lingo such as 'wicked' and 'Hi' ... She thought this a Hampstead colloquial phrase for beginning a letter. I wouldn't like to mention that half the people in this bloody country use it. But no matter. She's becoming ever more trendy every day!

Margaret had tried to persuade Adam to go and see a counsellor but his pride had stood in the way. Adam's death devastated her as much as it did me, and it bound us together. She loved him deeply and I know that she has battled with guilt, and the 'what ifs', ever since.

She wasn't able to save Adam but she saved me.

When I was okay, we did normal things. I drove her car and helped with the shopping. When the sadness overwhelmed me, Margaret sat with me. She allowed me to live my grief in whatever form it came, whenever it came. She lived it with me as she lived her own sadness. She sat with me hour after hour, allowed me to 'be' in all my agony and fear, so real that I had to touch it. In doing so, Margaret gave me the greatest gift. I ricocheted between London and Edinburgh, but the pain followed me. It hunted me down wherever I went, my constant predator.

Back in London, friends and neighbours smothered me with love and offers of help, yet I felt suffocated, as if they were projecting their own fear on to me, the fear that I would do to myself what Adam had done to himself. It felt that no one could handle my grief. Their fear fuelled my own.

What if what happened to Ad happened to me?

I could not yet see clearly that I had a choice: that suicide is an act of will, and that even in the darkest of moments I did not possess that wish to die. I wrote a letter to my friend in Japan

'I don't want to die but I don't know how to live ...'

The first Christmas without Adam was horrific. I felt the heaviness build up within me, layers of sodden earth swamping my soul. It was Christmas Eve, barely five weeks since that cold dark night of hell. I looked at my father crumpled in his chair. I knew I couldn't show him my pain. I couldn't do it to him. I had to get out, so I rang Jess and arranged to meet her and Dan at the pub. I just want to be normal, I thought, just a normal teenager.

At the pub I watched the air-kissing and the merriness and I wanted to vomit. The Christmas cheer there was even more suffocating than being at home in the grief-soaked silence with Dad. What made it worse was that I felt everyone looking at me, wondering what I was doing there, staring at me with pity. I wanted to scream, *'You have no fucking idea, so don't even pretend that you do, and don't come near me!'*

'Dan, I have to get out.'

'Whatever you want, Teej.'

I led him to Hampstead Heath, where I had so often walked with Adam. We all knew never to go there alone at night for several women had been raped. Even outside, in the open space, claustrophobia still boxed me in. It was 1.30am. We walked and walked, off the path, into tall grass, and trees. I dropped to my knees; my face crumpled and contorted, the tears within fighting to erupt. The tears morphed into a howl and finally into an earth-shattering scream that emanated from every cell in my body.

Whhhhhhhyyyyyyyyyyyyyyyy????

The ear-curdling shrieks reverberated into the silence. When my breath ran out I slumped into a pile on my knees, head and hands in the grass, feeling the damp coldness of the earth at my fingertips, and the word hung in the emptiness.

Dan sat quietly next to me. Someone in the distance stopped and turned. Should they help? Was another woman being raped? No, just a teenager caught in a tornado of grief.

I was a seventeen-year-old girl who did not yet know her own mind. I needed someone I could trust to tell me that I was normal, that I wasn't going mad. A friend's mum referred me to Dr Katzman. I don't know what he was – a psychiatrist, a psychologist, a psychoanalyst? I dreaded going to see him. If I was having a good day I didn't want to take myself *there*, to that place again. I felt uncomfortable, painfully so. *Can't you just say something?* I thought. *Just tell me I'm not mad and make it better?* I was racked with normal teenage insecurities, but grief amplified them.

While I hated seeing Dr Katzman, he did reassure me that I was not going mad. That everything I was feeling was normal, even the panic. I needed that to get me through.

After a while, I started to see a pattern: the build-up of heaviness and tension, followed by the inevitable eruption and release. The intensity of grief remained, but there were brief periods of dormancy that followed each explosion and I became thankful for that respite, even if it only lasted a few hours. I told myself over and over that if I could get through this, I could handle anything. What I didn't know was that surviving came at a cost, and it would be many years before I realized how my pathological fear of loss would manifest itself in my behaviour and relationships.

I'll always be here for you, Ta, Ad had scribbled in his note to me. With the knowledge that he wasn't, came the soul-crushing reality that no one could ever make that guarantee.

With time, I started to recognize that the only person I could depend on for comfort was me.

During my moments of respite I tried to study, for the only glimmer of light I could see in the darkness that otherwise consumed me was the possibility of my going to Zimbabwe with Operation Raleigh, and to do that I needed to pass my exams. After that, I would go to Edinburgh University, just as Adam had wished for me. The place he should have gone to himself.

Adam's chemistry teacher, Doc Woolley, offered to tutor me as I had missed so much of my final year. Adam's death had affected him deeply and he was aware of some of the conflict in my brother's mind since our mother's death.

I didn't understand chemistry. My teacher, thinking that I would surely fail the exam, had told me that I should wait a year. The thought of spending another year at home in London was intolerable, so every week I went to the chemistry lab at my brother's old school and Doc would stay back to tutor me. I was painfully aware of how I was no Adam, either academically or personally. I felt inadequate and unable to live up to Adam's abilities, intellect or compassion. A chemistry essay had been sitting on his desk at Balliol the night he jumped from his window. The teacher had scrawled on the front, 'This is possibly one of the finest essays written by a first-year student at Oxford that I have ever read.'

I sat at my desk, hour after hour, staring blankly at the files in front of me full of meaningless words and equations.

Please make the pain better – please.
What did I do to deserve this?
Why, Ad? Why? Why did you do this to me? I loved you with all my heart and it wasn't enough.
Oh, Mum – I wish you could just give me a big, big hug and tell me everything's going to be all right. I wish I was still that little five-year-old that used to hide behind your skirt.
I wish none of this had ever happened.
I just want my family back.
I want to feel loved.
I want to feel safe.
I want to be protected, cared for and looked after.
But I also want to be strong.
Six months and it's still here – all the pain, all the hurt.

In June, nine long months after Adam's death, I stepped out of my A-level chemistry exam. Jess and Dan came to pick me up in the old Mini Cooper Jess and I shared. Their faces beamed at me. 'Look, Teej! Dan performed a high-speed 360-degree turn, missing a bench by inches. He'd been perfecting the manoeuvre while they had been waiting, as a sort of fanfare for me. We laughed gleefully and I looked to the heavens.

'I survived! I'm free!'

Pain passes, grief passes, fear passes, panic passes.

They can also return.

The phone rang and I ran to it. I was so happy to have finished my exams.

'Hello.'

'Hello, could I speak to Adam Lal, please?'

'Sorry?' I faltered.

'Is that the number for Adam Lal? It's the police here. We need to interview him as a witness.'

'Adam's dead.' I shook as I said the words.

'Oh, oh, I'm so sorry. I'm so sorry to upset you.'

I put the phone down and I was there, in it again. Just like that. I started going through old papers and found a letter from the coroner who had returned various scraps of paper bearing my brother's familiar scrawl, his unfinished letters and his suicide note. The last few days of my brother's life, and his death, held together with a staple.

The one thing that I held on to was that Adam had wanted to die. But the notion that maybe, just maybe, he hadn't was unacceptable to me. His words rang in my head: *Want to die now. Well, I don't really …*

Hesitantly, I asked questions. Would he be alive if that old woman in the street had not said those thoughtless words? Would he be alive had he not been strip-searched at the airport? Would he be alive if I'd had more understanding, more insight? Would he be alive if his ex-girlfriends had not hurt him? Would he be alive if Dad had been able to be a father? Would he be alive if he'd never smoked pot or taken drugs? Would he be alive if Mum had not died? Did he die just because he was in the middle of a panic attack? The endless unanswered questions of suicide …

The only way to have any peace, so that I could live, was to tell myself that he *had* wanted to die.

I read all of Adam's diaries. Among the excerpts he had transcribed from DH Lawrence's books a sentence caught my eye: *TJ 'he put his hope in her'.* TJ was the name he often used for me. I seized Adam's words, threading them into my soul. I told myself that my brother had passed me a cup, full of his hopes. I grasped it eagerly. I had found my answer, my reason to live. I would live the life he could not. I would lead a useful, caring life just as Mum had wished. I would do it for Adam and myself. This is what carried me forward.

I didn't know when I grasped it, how heavy the cup would be.

PART TWO

Building a New Life

CHAPTER 15

Heathrow Airport, 3 October 1989

I stood in among the chaos of young exuberant travellers about to embark on their journeys, their families fussing attentively around them, surrounded by an army of backpacks. Anxiously, I looked around me, clinging to my own carefully packed rucksack as if it were a safety blanket. I was thankful my aunt had come to see me off, for I was eighteen years old and painfully shy, about to embark on an expedition to Zimbabwe. There was no one here that I knew.

It was almost exactly a year since I'd written so fervently to Adam at Oxford describing every last detail of my selection weekend. I knew he would have wanted me to do this. As the departure date had neared, however, I'd started to question myself. What if seeing all the poverty in Africa affected me as it had done Adam? What if I had a panic attack while I was away? It had been eleven months since Adam had died. What if I wasn't ready? The doubts nagged at me incessantly.

Yet as soon as I set eyes on the plains of Africa, something shifted in me. I felt a sense of awe, some sort of release from deep within me. We began setting up camp, building shacks and digging long-drop toilets, sleeping under our own hand-made shelters, just as Adam had. He had written:

There is something holy and comfortable and precious about sheltering under canvas while storms rage upon open hillsides, and here in the Himalayas of India there is definitely no exception to this idyll.

It did seem holy, for I felt a completeness I had not experienced before. When eight of us climbed into an inflatable dinghy embarking on three days of wild-water rafting, I looked up at the black jagged rocks of the Zambezi valley as they towered above us and I felt their dominance, aware of our own insignificant mortality. The water swelled around us, angrily crashing off the rocks, relentlessly immersing us in the raging torrent of water. Adam had written in his diary:

To see nature harness nature with such unbelievable force; rocks as if slain lie moist and greasy on the sponge-like earth. The streams appear to revel in the tempestuous air, seemingly to swell and rage in greater fury, daunting and menacing.

The very force of it seemed to free me from the mental anguish that had restrained me over the past months. Like Adam, I felt the power of nature. I began talking to people, engaging with them, even laughing.

I was posted to Chisuma, a remote village in the north-west of the country, composed primarily of mud huts with perfectly manicured roofs made of straw. It was an arid region marked by dry grassy plains, the occasional cactus and sparse shrubs that looked desperate to hold on to their few remaining leaves. We set about working with the local villagers to build a school block. Every morning I'd greet the locals with 'Mangwanani!' and we'd do the African handshake. I felt completely at ease, as if this was a part of me. A smiling black face with gleaming white teeth leant out of a rickety old bus.

'Yo there, black *seeestar*, we *luuuuurve* you!' he hollered at me. I smiled. At last I belonged.

✻

There were no machines here. We had only our bodies and some basic tools to rely on. Even the sand and gravel we needed to mix with the cement we sourced from local riverbeds and sifted by hand. I grasped the sand, feeling it run through my fingers, as if physically touching the earth was grounding me. I basked in the manual toil, the sweat and the sun. Digging trenches and making bricks became strangely soothing. It felt almost as if, in laying the foundations of the school block, I was also starting to rebuild the foundations of my life. I scribbled in my journal:

I just can't get over how relaxed I feel. I haven't felt this at ease or happy in years, perhaps ever. It feels like I'm doing everything I've always wanted to do. I'm outdoors, using my body, exercising and doing adventurous things. I'm surrounded by great people, part of a team and we all have a laugh. I'm away from the rat race and the pressures of home and London. It's great. My only regret is that Ad can't see all this. He'd have loved it here. I want to share it all with him, show him how good life can be, let him know that I'm happy and I love him.

We set out on a three-week trek across the Mavuradonha Mountains and the Zambezi escarpment, following elephant tracks. At night, we merely laid down a tarp and slept under the watchful eye of the stars. Unknowingly, I walked in Adam's footsteps, for he had written:

We sat around the flickering flames enjoying the warmth of the group circle. The light enlivened laughter, the sanguinity of the red embers and the happiness in shared experience made it a wonderful evening so carefree and blissful ...

We carried our food supplies with us and relied on rivers for water. One evening I sat washing my dirt-caked clothes in a stream, just as Adam had done, smiling as I thought of my brother and his words:

There I sat, bum perched on a bumpy rock beside a miserable trickle of a stream. Soak the socks, sprinkle a few valuable grains of travel wash on them and slap them against a flat rock. It followed like a recipe – true Indian style minus the soap powder. It was incredible how pleasant it was. I could have sat there for hours in the fresh morning sun.

I learned to use a compass to navigate the peaks and valleys of the terrain, or perhaps I was learning to navigate life. We took it in turns to lead, searching always for a trough where we might find water. The sun beat down relentlessly as we battled though the vegetation, ambushed by wild shrubs that seemed to be intent on leaving their itchy mark on us, smiling as they injected their poison. Our legs gave way beneath us as we lumbered on clumsily, just as Adam had written:

Again we panted, sweated and wheezed our way up tortuously steep slopes that wove onward and onward toward the summit.

My two water bottles ran dry, as did those of the others in the group. I was buoyed only by the knowledge of an impending river as we began to descend.

The descent is slow and tricky through the valleys of sun-parched rock. The skin on your feet blisters against your permanently angled shoes, all the while fighting off the savage rays of the scorching sun.

We neared the base of the valley, watching as it stared back at us in arid defiance, as parched as our mouths. I looked up at the steep ascent ahead of us, my skin inflamed and red, mouth as dry as the ground on which I stood. Fear began to rumble within me. We discussed, and rejected, drinking our own urine. Instead we began to dig for water, deeper and deeper, eventually watching the dark liquid ooze from the earth. We sifted the muddy silt-ridden water through a cloth, putting a few drops of iodine in it. I took a deep breath, closed my eyes and drank.

In that brown murky water I tasted life. I became stripped of everything, all the grief, the despair, the hopelessness; everything that I needed was in that water. On we hiked ...

We slipped and slid our way across the snow mounds in the usual silence that always accompanies a group while it walks. It is a highly personal silence in which thoughts wander with blissful fluidity. Time appears to evaporate rather than pass. It is a contented peace that rests upon a worry-free brain. No fear, no anxiety, no schedule to meet. The big city seems so far away as if, locked in this distant dream, lie all your troubles. Your heart and mind are truly tranquil. How far away did London anxiety seem from me now? Peace and calm prevailed, soothing and pleasant.

Like Adam, I found peace in the mountains. I found the methodical rhythm of it soothing, climbing for hours, winding our way through the bush ... *cocooned in silence gazing at the spectacular scenery in a satisfied contented temper.* No words spoken, trudging, aching, yet bathed in an extraordinary calmness. I came to value the silence, to treasure it, just as my brother had done.

Then of course there was the silence: sweet, beautiful peace. To sit there thinking of freedom with the 'eloquence of silence'.

In Zimbabwe I found peace in the simplicity of life. I found liberation in the knowledge that everything I needed was on my back or in the earth on which I stood. I gained a sense of standing on solid ground once more. At last a light shone on my path, allowing me a different vantage point. I could see my life before me with genuine enthusiasm and passion, for Adam and I were walking our paths together.

I have often thought that my life has travelled not from birth toward death but from death toward life. It is as if my journey started beneath the ground in darkness, without air to breathe, blindly clawing through the soil toward the quicksand, crawling toward life on hands and knees. I've fallen into wild rivers, I've trudged through forests and moorland, clambered over ridges and up to peaks, only to stumble over cliffs and into crevasses. At times I've travelled a well-defined path, at others the path is steep and unclear and I am easily lost. On occasion, a bridge has appeared as a welcome gift; at other times cloud has obscured all that lies before me. Zimbabwe lit my way, enabling me to take a step up out of the morass.

CHAPTER 16

My return to London began with a classic 'Dad episode'. Jo had driven my father to Heathrow airport in my beaten-up old Mini Cooper. She was flying out to the States that day to see her American boyfriend and she warned me at the airport that I would have to push-start the car.

I piled my backpack stuffed full of African mementos into the car, placing my treasured soapstone elephant carefully under the seat. A wooden giraffe head peered out of my pack, grinning at me from the back seat. Dad hadn't driven since Mum banned him after he nearly killed my sister all those years ago so I explained to him how he would have to push the car while I steered.

I sat in the driver's seat, assuming my father would position himself at the back of the car.

'Okay, go, Dad,' I said.

I waited.

'Go, Dad,' I repeated.

I heard a grunt, just as I began to feel the car rocking beneath me, side to side. I turned my head, my jaw dropping as I was greeted by the sight of my father standing at the side of the car, rocking it, with his entire might.

'Dad, Dad ... the wheels go *that* way, as in forward and back, not sideways!' I took a deep breath. 'You have to push from behind,' I said, exasperated.

'Ah … I see, I see,' Dad muttered.

Here we go, I thought trying to hold the peace I had in Zimbabwe, just as Adam had done on his return.

Well, I'm back in London. Gone is the sense of freedom and in place are the social rules of heart and mind.

I got a job waiting tables at a restaurant. Given my clumsy penchant for smashing plates, it was never going to be a smooth journey. After several mishaps involving the tipping of red wine onto white designer jackets and hot coffee poured into an unassuming young gentleman's lap, the owners politely suggested I might like to work in their delicatessen instead. So I ate my way through my days in the deli and forced myself to stick at waiting tables there.

I was determined to hold on to some of the confidence I had built in Zimbabwe. I made myself interact with people, to look them in the eye and make conversation. I started ever so slowly to connect with people at a very basic level. It felt as if I was peeling away just a tiny part of the layer that shielded me, and that made me happy because I liked people. I just didn't know how to let them see 'me', but maybe I didn't know who 'me' was.

I saved money and travelled to Indonesia and Japan on my own, determined to prove my independence, which I did, all the while craving company. I used to look wistfully at all the groups of young friends travelling together, having fun. I wanted to be like them, to be a part of it. I was so happy to return home in June 1990 in time for Jo's wedding. The ceremony was held in the same church that Mum and Dad had been married in, the same church where I'd stood staring at my mum's coffin as a thirteen-year-old, and the same church that had overflowed with grief at Adam's funeral. At last we smiled and shed tears of joy in that church. After the wedding Jo moved to the United States. Once again, it was just me and Dad.

❁

I went up to Edinburgh to start my university life, just as Adam had hoped I would. I recalled the letter he had scrawled to me when he left for Oxford to embark on his own university days. It felt good to know that I was doing what he had wanted.

In Edinburgh, I lived like a typical student, eating baked beans on toast and shivering my way through winter, gauging the temperature in my bedroom by my ability to see my breath in the morning when I lay in bed. I could see Arthur's Seat out of my bedroom window. Well, I could once the frost on it had melted. I drank copious amounts of beer and smoked a few cigarettes in between learning to windsurf and play basketball. In short, I did everything except study. In fact, I prided myself when I managed to get a negative mark in my first-year quantitative mathematics exam, by virtue of the fact that it was a multiple-choice exam in which a mark was deducted for every wrong answer you gave. I giggled at my achievement, laughing with my newfound friends. I visited my aunt for cups of tea, and she invariably asked me if I had been burning the candle at both ends, seeing the grey rings around my eyes. During my holidays I waited tables and travelled anywhere and everywhere I could, taking student loans out to fund my trips.

Although the years after Mum had died had been lost to me, my twenties were lived in a blissful, unaware kind of way. In short, I took time out from grief, blind but happy.

Shortly after my twenty-first birthday, I met a guy called Jonny at the Commonwealth swimming pool in Edinburgh, which was just up the road from my flat. I used to meet my friend Anna there after our afternoon lectures. One day, I'd hauled myself out of the pool, bored of ploughing up and down the black line. I wished my friend farewell and left. The next day, as I sat myself down next to Anna for our biochemistry lecture, she whispered to me.

'My friend Jonny wants to meet you! He saw you getting out of the pool. He's got it bad!'

I was flattered. Jonny was older than me. He drove a nice black car. He seemed like a man not a boy, tall and big with beautiful blue eyes and a slightly receding hairline. It wasn't long before we started dating. I loved to get myself lost in his big hairy chest. He always said to me that he reckoned all the hair had fallen off his head and landed on his chest. We had fun together, living the student life.

I really liked him and I liked being in a relationship. It felt good to be loved, and I knew he did love me. At times he'd tell me I was distant, or get frustrated that I didn't show him more affection. I told him I loved him, for I assumed I did, but somewhere deep inside, I felt at odds.

I didn't hold the strength or purity of feeling for him that I had for Adam. I would have done anything in the world for Adam, yet I didn't feel that way for Jonny. Did that mean I didn't love him? At times I preferred to watch TV rather than be with him. He frustrated me. I started to question if what I felt was really love.

We spent three years together, yet in that entire time we never really spoke of my past, of Adam and Mum, or any of the heartache that I had felt. I had packed it all safely away in the deepest recesses of my heart so that I barely felt its existence. I didn't know then that you tend to fall over the things you put behind you, as if they are constantly drawing you back, until you finally turn around to look at what's there and revisit the past.

One day, during my third year at Edinburgh, when I had started wondering what I was going to do with a degree in physiology, I sat myself down in front of a computer-generated careers program. Diligently I filled in question after question about my likes and dislikes, my priorities and passions. After an hour or so, the computer obligingly spat out a list of fitting professions:

1. Fireman. (Gender political correctness clearly hadn't arrived in Edinburgh in 1993.)
2. Physiotherapist.

I laughed. Fireman? I'd never thought of that. Physiotherapy? Now that seemed like the perfect fit. I could engage my fascination with the human body and stay connected to sport while making a difference to people's lives.

I completed my degree with honours in physiology, although how I passed I'll never know. I began looking for courses to study physiotherapy. But I still had a thirst for travel. I wanted to see the world and be free. I didn't want to be tied to Jonny any more, so I ended my relationship with him in a heartless, distant kind of a way, had a brief fling with a friend of mine and threw myself into endless hours of waiting tables to save the money for my trip. I actually became a half-decent waitress in the end, proving to myself that anything's possible if you practise.

Finally, in February 1995, I left England grasping a one-year round-the-world air ticket. I travelled through Thailand and the Philippines before arriving in Sydney on 28 March. I always remember this date because it is the date I found my home.

CHAPTER 17

I was twenty-four when I flew into Sydney on a perfect autumn day and caught my first glimpse of the harbour with its luminescent Opera House, flaunting its beauty, luring me in, toward the light. I could see the white triangles of tiny yachts, like stars on the sparkling water. I took a deep breath. It felt surreal. I was finally here, the place I'd dreamed and read about for so many years.

Mum had been to Australia with work, researching documentaries, before she married. She had named a teddy bear of mine Sydney, and since her death I had kept a toy koala that had been her good-luck mascot. He had gone everywhere with me, anywhere I might need luck. He'd sat on my desk through my school exams, had come to every athletics meet I'd ever attended, and he was there with me whenever I cried. It had never occurred to me that he was a koala or that he came from Australia. He was with me because he had been Mum's, and I wanted to hold something of hers.

It was only years later, when my aunt told me that Mum had loved Australia and had dreamed of moving there one day, that the pieces fell into place. I looked at my koala, thought of my teddy named Sydney and smiled. It gave me a sense of destiny, of things happening for a reason. All would unfold just as it should.

❁

I got a job waiting tables in a restaurant that sat directly under the Opera House. It was almost surreal walking through Circular Quay every day, watching the army of ferries and jet cats chug in and out busily. As I walked toward the sails of the Opera House I would gaze at the Harbour Bridge as it hung over the lively blue water that almost seemed to talk to me, willing me to stay. Countless times, as I laid a plate of pre-theatre food down in front of a customer, I would glance up, stealing a glimpse of the water and the bridge and smile in disbelief. I was a part of the postcards that I'd stared longingly at for so many years, living and breathing it.

To earn some extra money, I got a job as a drinks waitress at the Basement, a live music venue near Circular Quay. That's where I met Anthony.

I remember the first time I saw him. He was standing behind the bar in his black Basement T-shirt. He had beautiful olive skin, thick dark hair and piercing blue eyes.

'Hey, I'm Anthony. Anything you need, just ask,' he said with genuine enthusiasm and a sparkle in his eye.

He took my breath away. Somehow, though, he made me feel relaxed. Nothing seemed to bother him. He always seemed to have time for me. If I forgot a drink order, he'd just throw his hands in the air and say, 'Pretty sure it was a gin and tonic, eh?' with a cheeky glint in his eye that melted my anxiety into a loving smile.

Unlike me, he never seemed to stress about anything. When I asked which cappuccino was skim, he'd just grin and whirl a finger in the air before pointing at whichever one took his fancy, exclaiming, 'This one!' I would just shake my head and laugh, praying the customer didn't have some full-fat milk allergy.

As staff we often sat and had a drink after work. It was the highlight of my day, a chance to get to know Anthony a bit better. He was always chatty and friendly. Everyone seemed to love him. It was impossible not to be drawn to his playful boyish nature. In his characteristic laid-back way, he always wanted to help people, fixing their cars and offering everyone, including me, a lift home after work. Like me, he lived in Bondi.

I hid my adoration in every way I could, convinced that Anthony was not interested in me. We talked many times of the virtues of friendship over romance, which I took as his way of letting me know that he wasn't keen. I was the world's most useless flirter. Whatever one is supposed to do in order to let a man know that you're attracted to him, I am sure I did the opposite. When Anthony offered me a lift home I would cheerfully decline and hop on the bus. When he looked me in the eye, I would look away. And whenever the subject of romance came up, I said how great it was to have male friends.

We arranged to go indoor rock climbing. He picked me up outside Town Hall station in his green Toyota Corolla. Samantha, Anthony's sister, sat in the passenger seat. I'm not sure what I thought his sister would be like, but she wasn't supposed to be that beautiful. My nervousness mounted. Sam was wearing a tiny crop top and shorts that sat perfectly on her slim, tanned hips. She was gorgeous and trendy. I felt huge in my big baggy Mambo T-shirt. *Oh God*, I thought. *If you have a sister like that, why would you like me?*

I sat in the back seat of the car, staring lustfully at the back of Anthony's neck, wishing I could reach out and touch it. But I didn't, and nothing happened after that. *I'm okay with friends*, I thought.

Life jumbled along happily, working at the Opera House and the Basement, living nocturnally. I was sharing a flat in Bondi with other backpackers, living in milk-crate city. Did you know that milk crates make great chests of drawers, coffee tables, stools and bookshelves? My fifty dollars per week rent to share a room in milk-crate city even included bills. I'd never saved so much money in my life. Having no real responsibilities gave me an invigorating sense of freedom. All my troubles and my pain were neatly and conveniently packed away back in England.

I had planned to work for three months, save money and travel before heading back to London, but I had a one-year visa, and life was good. I didn't want to go home. I don't think it ever occurred to me that my decision to stay on in Sydney might have an impact on anyone else. Anyway, nothing was going to stop me staying where I could be carefree and pain-free.

I called Jo.

'Hi, Jo, I think I'm going to stay here for a while, cash in my air ticket and use up my visa.'

'What? What about the house, Ta? We need to clear it all out to sell it. I'm not bloody doing it all on my own, you know,' she said, angry and exasperated, for she had realized the enormity of clearing out thirty years' worth of accumulated belongings.

We had an attic full of memories and endless boxes full of Mum and Adam's clothes, letters and things we hadn't known what to do with. I was supposed to be there too. Jo needed my help.

It was a bad time for her. Her marriage had broken up and she was deeply unhappy. I never really knew what had happened. Whether it was because she chose not to tell me, or because I failed to ask, I do not know. It didn't occur to me how acutely painful a marriage break-up would be, and Jo never liked to show her vulnerability so we never talked about it. By now our lives were worlds apart, emotionally as well as geographically. I put down the phone, ignoring my sister's plea for help.

Then I rang Jonny to tell him the news. He put the phone down on me. We had broken up, but I realize that he was still holding out hope. He was waiting for me to come home. I had no idea of the pain I caused him.

I cashed in my return ticket and continued my carefree existence.

6 August 1995

After work, we sat around the bar at the Basement having a staff drink. It would have been Mum's sixty-third birthday, as well as Mum and Dad's twenty-ninth wedding anniversary.

One of the bar girls, Pip, came over to me.

'Are you ever going to get together with Anthony? Because, you know, if you want it, it's there,' she said nonchalantly.

I was speechless. Had he said something to her? Was she sure?

Anthony gave me a lift home that night and we sat on Bondi beach like a pair of schoolkids, fiddling with the sand, staring at the water.

'I feel like a kid,' he said.

I laughed nervously, 'Yeah ... playing in the sand.'

He smiled. We both knew he hadn't meant that at all. Rather that he felt like a teenager on a first date.

I focused even more intently on the sand, until finally I looked up and he kissed me.

'I can't believe I just did that,' he said with the childish innocence that I loved.

From that moment we were inseparable and all the shared paranoia and misconceptions of the last few months came tumbling out. We laughed like teenagers about all our misconstrued conversations. I felt just as I'd always dreamed I would. It was everything I'd always imagined falling in love to be. I was head over heels and so was he.

At work, Anthony just stood staring at me and I would smile back, abashed by the intensity in his eyes. One morning, soon after the night on Bondi beach, I woke up in his flat to hear him shouting from the street below the window. I stuck my head out. There was Anthony holding a red rose. I beamed a love-struck smile.

'I'm coming up!'

His apartment was on the second floor of an old redbrick block on busy Bondi road, the main thoroughfare to the beach. Anthony put the rose between his teeth and began to climb as cars and buses trundled by. He scaled the side of that building with only his bare fingers and toes. I laughed and shook my head. A guy walked past and shouted:

'Eh mate ... Want a ladder?'

We had a fair audience by the time he finally made it to the window and into my arms. They chuckled about young love. And it was, young, innocent, lustful, uncomplicated love.

❋

I felt totally safe with Anthony. If I was upset, he always held me, reassuring and comforting me even if he had no idea what was wrong.

'It's going to be okay, bub, I promise, it's all going to be okay,' he would say gently as he hugged me. He had an amazing ability to make me believe him. I felt warm and safe.

He took me to meet his parents soon after they had moved to the Blue Mountains, west of Sydney. I didn't know that he had described me to his mother as an Indian princess. She opened the door, expecting to see a petite Indian girl with slender features, and was somewhat surprised when she saw me, tall, muscular and Amazonian with a mass of curly hair. Having recovered from the initial shock, Anthony's parents, Helga and Bert, invited me into their family with open arms. 'Don't you dare hurt that girl,' his father warned Anthony.

I could not have anticipated then the bond I would form with Anthony's family or the impact they would have on my life. I had thought I had found the love of my life. In fact what I found was so much more.

As my visa neared its expiry date so the pressure mounted to make a plan for the future. There seemed so many obstacles in our way. We had been together for less than six months. Could we really make a commitment to move to the other side of the world after such a short time? I wanted an answer; I craved certainty.

Anthony never planned ahead. He had a sense that every-thing would work out. Had he asked and pleaded, I would have married him on the spot, but he didn't. One night, after I had been pushing hard for an answer, we had an argument. I walked out of the pub we were in. Anthony followed me all the way home, walking patiently behind me for over an hour, never letting me out of his sight.

Finally we agreed he would come over to England for a holiday and we would see what happened. I left Australia the day my visa ran out and I cried and cried. I spent six weeks in New Zealand on my way back to England, sneaking to the phone whenever I could to speak to Anthony, and writing letters when I couldn't get to a phone. I filled my days with every adventure sport I could think of. I sky-dived, white-water rafted, bungee-jumped, ice-climbed, took helicopter rides and hiked my way around the country. I was back in the mountains, in my element, where, like Adam, I always felt most at peace. He'd written:

Every panorama possesses a snow-capped mountain whose sides appear etched by a sculptor's chisel, so naked and sharp are the rocks that form them. Clouds float in oblivious bliss through and among the peak – puffy and white – the type in which one finds faces. But perhaps one of the most spectacular sights of the day occurred when we had clawed our way up to the top of Cathedral and were timidly looking down the other side into a mountain crevasse where a stream raged but appeared to murmur. Two eagles floated in the air currents that rose from the valley floor. There is no need for me to describe the scene further as it is one so often recounted but so rarely seen – the majesty of the birds and their effortless grace soaring high and far in the mountain air – it was fantastic. We were on a par with the eagles.

I stood at the top of a ridge on the Routeburn Track, looking out at the spectacular scene before me, feeling an invigorating sense of freedom. That night I nestled in my sleeping bag in among the peace and tranquillity of the mountains in one of the tiny wooden huts that lined the track. I drifted into sleep, only to awake in the middle of the night. I became immediately aware of a deep rumbling within my soul that sat at odds with the quiet contented breathing of my fellow travellers. It felt as if a predator were preparing to strike. Fear clamped my chest, scaling the walls of my throat, stealing the breath from me until the panic engulfed me. I fought for logic. *Why now? Why is this happening?* The more I looked for answers the faster the fear spread. I felt as if I were in a cage, dangling precariously somewhere above the world, looking down at it wistfully. It was as if one of Adam's eagles had caught me unawares, swooping down to grip me with its claws, severing my link with reality, driving me down into a crevasse.

The panic robbed me of my connection to the present moment, as if it sliced the cord that bound me to the world and to nature. It brought me face to face with my deepest fear: that I would lose my mind just as I had watched my brother lose his fight and my father struggle continuously in the battle for his sanity.

It had been eight years since Adam's death, but the panic attack was a signal that all was not well within my soul. Adam's words echoed in the mountain air:

It used to come from my heart and then I put it away and never looked at it again. Now it's back, the vigour and truth of within.

I was on my way back to London, returning to the painful truth of all that I had packed away deep in my heart for the last fifteen months. I didn't want to confront what lay ahead, or what lay behind. I flew into Heathrow and I looked around me. The people seemed strained and grey-faced, just like the weather. I walked back into the darkness of my memories.

CHAPTER 18

I lay in my familiar bed at home in our house in London. I thought of Anthony and I started to sob. I missed him so much. Our family house was on the market and I had made an offer on a flat in London, which had been accepted. I had a place confirmed on a physiotherapy course. I should have been happy, but my heart wasn't in it. Dad had come to visit to sort through his books before we sold the house. I heard his familiar heavy footsteps ascending the stairs, coming to rest outside my bedroom door.

'Ah … Tara … Are you all right?' Dad asked, anxiety and concern lacing every word.

'I'm just upset, Dad. It's okay,' I said, trying to stifle my sobs for I never wanted to worry him.

He didn't open the door. He didn't come in. Instead we held the entire conversation through my closed bedroom door, with him standing on the landing.

'I … I … just don't know what to do, Dad.' I hiccupped through my tears. 'I love Anthony,' I said tentatively, for I rarely showed my emotion to my father.

There was a quiet pause before my father's soft voice filtered through the closed door.

'Follow your heart, Tara.' His words echoed in the room.

It was a rare moment of clarity and connection between us that transcended the closed door, a treasured gift of wisdom from my father. The finest he had ever given me.

❀

I was waiting tables in a restaurant in Camden Town while I waited for Anthony to arrive. I couldn't wait to see him. He had cut his trip through South-East Asia short because he missed me. I went to meet him at Gatwick airport still head over heels in love. He appeared through the sliding doors wearing a faded red woven shirt and his old ragged jeans, backpack slung across his shoulders. Just as he had when I first saw him, he took my breath away. The frenzied hectic bustle of the arrivals lounge at Gatwick became only a distant fuzzy haze as we embraced, enclosed in our own world. God, I loved this man.

It was less than twenty-four hours before Anthony asked me to come back to live in Australia with him. It was the moment I'd been waiting for. I didn't even hesitate in saying yes. I had my father's blessing. I was going to go and live in Australia with Anthony.

By the time I had returned from my travels Jo had already cleared a lot of the stuff out of the attic in our house. With hindsight I realized how unsupported she must have felt doing it on her own. I had happily shunned the responsibility until I'd returned home. It is the decision-making that cripples you. What to keep and what to chuck? Everything has a memory, an emotion, attached to it.

Together Jo and I spent many hours in the loft sifting through family memories. Do you read every letter you find? Do you keep your dead mother's wedding dress? Do you keep your dead brother's schoolbooks? Do you take the risk and throw away boxes of papers and cards that you haven't had time to look at? I was paralysed: *What if I chuck my brother's schoolbook and it has something important in it? What if he'd scribbled a poem?*

There was a permanency about throwing things away that stank of death. Yet a part of me wanted to rid myself of everything, as if that way I might shed the pain too, so that I could start my life afresh.

Jo and I became more ruthless as time went by. Our motto became 'fuck it, chuck it'. Painfully and slowly we cleared our family house. Eventually the 'For sale' sign was replaced by a 'Sold' one.

When the time came to move out, the stress and resentment had built to such an extent between Jo and me that it boiled over into a full-scale screaming match. My annoying habit of crying, something I couldn't seem to control, only made things worse. I cried when I was sad; I cried when I was angry. It was frustrating that when I wanted to show my anger, the tears always seemed to get there first.

We started arguing about where the removal truck was going to park. I became increasingly frustrated, and then the tears came. Jo knew exactly which button to push.

'That's right, cry like you always do,' she snarled from the top of the stairs.

Something in me snapped, an overwhelming rage enveloping my body.

'I fucking hate you. You stupid, horrible, ugly bitch!' I screamed at the top of my lungs, using every muscle in my body. I couldn't think of what I wanted to say or why, only that I hated her and wanted to hurt her in any way I could. A feeling born of a deep resentment for every hurt she had ever caused me or my brother. Now I laugh at those words. Ugly? Was that the best I could come up with? My sister is in fact very beautiful. A piece of cheese came hurtling toward me from my sister's hand in retaliation.

It was the only time I have ever shouted in rage at another person and the intensity of it shocked me. Anthony and Nic, my sister's boyfriend, looked at each other nervously from their respective corners. Eventually Anthony suggested gently that I should talk to Jo.

'I'm not speaking to that fucking bitch,' I replied with venom.

'Ta ...' he said, raising an eyebrow, taken aback by the uncharacteristic rage in my voice.

Finally the anger dissolved into sadness. The day we moved, Jo and I stood in the living room of our empty house, our childhood home. We hugged each other. It was a relief to say goodbye to the house: it held too much pain for us all. Without it to tie us together, my sister, my dad and I were free to live our own lives.

Anthony left for Australia five months before me. His father had avidly researched university places for me and as a result I had a place to study physiotherapy at Sydney University as an international student. Unfortunately my visa didn't start until January. I couldn't bear the thought of being apart for all that time so I went to the Australian high commission in the Strand, armed with a battery of reasons as to why I needed to be in Australia before my course started in February.

The man at the immigration counter looked at me, his face deadpan, and said, 'No.' I tried to explain that I hadn't a family or home here any more, that I had thrown everything away that I owned, except for six cardboard boxes full of photos and my brother's letters and diaries. I started crying.

'Please!'

He softened slightly. 'Go away and get yourself together,' he said. 'Come back to me in an hour.'

I ran out of the building and straight to the nearest phone box. I looked in my wallet. Only two pound coins. It was 1.30am in Sydney. I called the Basement and the manager answered.

'Please can you get Anthony? It's urgent.'

He put me on hold and I watched as the pennies ticked away. *Please hurry, please hurry.* Then I heard Anthony's voice.

'Bub, what's up?'

'They won't let me come. They won't give me a visa!' I sobbed into the phone.

'It's going to be okay, bub. I promise. I'll come over. I'll come and get you.'

Then the phone went dead. Hearing Anthony's voice had made me feel safe, in the way my mother had always done, and I walked back to the Australian high commission feeling calmer.

'Okay. You can have a three-month temporary visa, which will cover you before the start of your student visa, so long as you don't undertake paid work in that time.'

'I promise! I promise I won't work. Thank you. Thank you so much!'

I wanted to hug and kiss him. I had my ticket to get out of here. I was on my way to my new life, leaving the darkness behind.

The day before I left, I embarked on my last nose-to-armpit trip on the London underground in rush hour. *I'm sure as hell not going to miss this*, I thought.

I walked along Camden Road wondering how many thousands of times I must have walked the same path, and how this might be the last time. I felt an object skim past the top of my head. It was an empty Coke can that someone had chucked from the top of a double-decker bus as it crawled up the road.

That's right, T, I thought. *Get the hell out of this shithole.*

I glanced to my right as I walked past the newsagent's shop and caught the eye of a young man. I thought nothing of it and continued up the road. Ten minutes later, he came running up behind me, out of breath. 'I just wanted to tell you I think you're beautiful,' he puffed, and handed me a red rose.

I smiled. 'Thank you.'

'Do you live here?'

'Yes … no … sort of. I'm going to live in Australia. I leave tomorrow.'

'Oh, well, good luck. You're beautiful!'

That was it. He turned on his heel and walked back the way he had come. Life is full of contradictions, I thought. Maybe London wasn't so bad after all.

Dad and Jo took me to the airport. The tears flowed as I said goodbye and we hugged each other. Then Paul Hogan walked past and my sister and I cracked up laughing. I cried steadily in the plane, until somewhere over Russia, the tears stopped, replaced by a sense of excitement for my new life. A new beginning.

CHAPTER 19

I arrived at Sydney airport to be greeted not only by Anthony, but by Helga, Sam and Bert as well. They showered me with love, welcoming me into their open arms. I felt instantly that I had a new family, smiling at the familiarity as we drove down Bondi road on the way to Anthony's flat. Past the footy oval on the right and Three Steps greasy cafe (the best fry-up in town) and Harry's Pizza, the scene of many a drunken midnight feast. I glimpsed the ocean ahead of me, feeling a tingle of excitement into my stomach. A sense of warmth descended upon me. I knew then that I was home.

I started my degree in physiotherapy, studying hard and waiting tables at night to support myself. This was a degree I was going to use and I was passionate about my course-work, knowing I was heeding my mother's dying words: *I hope you will lead a useful and caring life.* I did nothing but study, work and spend time with Anthony. I didn't have any particularly close friends at this time. I didn't need to. I had him.

Anthony and I started collecting the necessary paperwork together for my application for Australian residency. I was applying on the grounds of our de facto relationship, and we had statutory declarations from friends and family members that our relationship was 'genuine and ongoing'; joint bank account statements showing that I had put the proceeds from the sale of the London house in both of our names; the letters we had written to each other in the months that we were apart; and a note of the joint lease we had taken on an apartment in Bondi. The stresses of day-to-day life began to mount. We weren't as carefree as we had been.

I rarely thought of or talked about my past; there were no reminders here, and no one knew my family. Life just ticked along. I was focusing increasingly on my university studies and Anthony was trying to break into the field of sound engineering. Music was his passion and he was still living the nocturnal life, so we gradually saw less of each other. By the time he crawled into bed at night I was fast asleep.

Still, though, on the surface everything seemed fine … except the panic attacks were back.

A friend of mine, Libby, with whom I'd waited tables in London, came over from England. She was disarmingly attractive and charming and she'd been going out with the extremely wealthy owner of the restaurant we both worked in. I felt intimidated by her in every way, aware of my inadequacies. I was flattered when she accepted my offer of a room in our flat and secretly thought how much a few extra dollars would help. She offered us rent but I didn't have the heart to take her money, at least until she'd found a job. Eventually Anthony and I found her waitressing work at the Basement. The topic of rent never came up again after that and we all seemed to get along well. Anthony still worked at the Basement at weekends so I often heard the two of them come home late after work, trying to be quiet as they listened to music and laughed. I heard them whisper as I tried to sleep. I didn't feel a part of it. I trusted Anthony completely but something felt uncomfortable. I could feel him drifting away from me.

Before long we stopped sleeping together. I became used to only ever seeing his smooth olive-skinned back in bed. I was always reluctant to try to tempt him into making love for fear he should reject me. My uneasiness morphed into a festering sense of nausea that began to envelop me. Finally, I looked Anthony in the eye one day and took myself by surprise with the words that came from my mouth.

'Are you in love with Libby?' I asked tentatively.

He gave a kind of half laugh and said, 'One English girl is enough for me.'

I trusted him so I let it go.

Then, two weeks before my second-year exams, we sat in our bedroom talking. Out of the blue, Anthony said, 'I don't think I love you any more.'

At that, my world disintegrated before my eyes.

There was no more comfort in Anthony's arms, only tears and isolation. I cried incessantly. Anthony couldn't cope with the devastation he saw in me, knowing he was the cause of it. He asked his mum to look after me. So, I went up to the mountains into Helga's open arms.

'It doesn't matter what happens, you are a part of the family,' she said as she wrapped me in a motherly hug, quietly muttering, 'I'll throttle that son of mine.'

I tried to study, but invariably I simply stared at the pages in front of me as tears rolled down my cheeks, dripping on to my notes, smudging the writing. I had flashbacks to sitting at my desk in London after Adam died, staring at my A-level notes through oceans of tears.

One day Helga asked me, with an uncharacteristic edge of spite in her voice: 'Tell me, does this have something to do with that friend of yours?'

'No, no,' I said, wondering if it did.

I sat my exams still crying; the two seemed to go hand in hand. Anthony went to stay at a friend's place and I returned to our apartment. Libby comforted me day after day. Every morning I would drive slowly down the road in the hope that I might see Anthony, that maybe it wasn't over. Eventually, when my exams were finished I met up with him.

'I don't understand what happened,' I said. 'When did you stop loving me? Why didn't you say something sooner?' I pleaded, desperate for answers.

He looked guilty. He never could lie to me.

'I kissed Libby one night,' he said.

'What?' I said, devastated. 'When? What happened?'

'It was only once, after work. We never slept together.'

With that my illusions of love disintegrated, just as Adam's had when his relationship with his girlfriend fell apart.

I don't really want to talk about Sarah because I see no reason to. I'm not upset in any way really, just, I suppose, somewhat weary. I'm fed up. I think my dreams of pure hearts and thoughts are rapidly encompassing themselves in just that, the world of the mind. Reality readily blasts them away, so kindly disposing of them as nonsense.

I wasn't angry with Anthony. I couldn't be angry with him because I still loved him and in my childlike mind anger and love could not co-exist. I reasoned that at least he had told me. Instead, I felt a deep sense of betrayal toward my friend who had comforted me only hours after she had kissed my boyfriend. Everything was her fault. She had flirted with Anthony, told him everything he wanted to hear, handed him a beautiful fantasy in a cup. I channelled every bit of anger toward her, telling her to get out of my flat even though I knew she had nowhere to go.

Anthony and I went to see a counsellor, at my request; I was desperate to save our relationship. We only went once. The counsellor questioned me about my family, and he kept going back to it, over and over again.

'It's not about my family,' I thought. 'It's about me and Anthony.'

I had happily packed up my pain in a box when I left England. I was not about to open it up now.

We told ourselves that we couldn't afford any more counselling.

The disintegration of our relationship escalated the moment my trust had been broken. I no longer believed Anthony when he said everything would be okay. Without the safety blanket he had always provided, our differences quickly became obvious.

When Anthony and I met, an unconscious force drew us to each other like powerful magnets. I grounded him and he cared for and comforted me. Only now do I question whether our relationship was one of mutual need packaged, ever so convincingly, as love. Or did our attraction morph into need? I don't know. One thing I do know is that I didn't love myself. In fact, I didn't even know myself, so how could I truly love another? I had no idea of the faulty ideas I held about what love was.

CHAPTER 20

Anthony and I remained friends, for I continued to love him. I simply could not let go of him entirely. The thought of him not being a part of my life was intolerable. I turned toward studying and a new job waiting tables. I began putting my life together again, oblivious to other men.

It wasn't long after Anthony and I had broken up that Luke, a bouncer at the Basement, invited me over to his place for drinks. He used to drop in to Sports Bar, the restaurant in Bondi where I worked, just to say hello. I often wondered why he was there. To me it always seemed a touch awkward. Luke was tall and big built, with small blue eyes and short sandy-coloured hair. He was very different to Anthony, always well dressed and groomed, reserved and shy. At times it could be hard to get conversation out of him. With Anthony, on the other hand, it was hard to get a word in edgeways. He was passionate and fiery while Luke was placid and quiet. He reminded me of a teddy bear, which I found endearing. We didn't really have a lot in common, but I liked him.

On the day of Luke's invite, I had a couple of drinks after work, trying to postpone going to his place, not sure of what to expect. So when I arrived rudely late, I was somewhat embarrassed to find only Luke and his best friend and his girlfriend there. I had thought it was just a casual thing. Feeling uncomfortable, I tucked into a few more beers. When Luke's friend and girlfriend got up to leave, I assumed it was time for me to go too. His friend looked at me surprised, as if to say, 'Aren't you staying?' It was only at that moment that it occurred to me that maybe this was a date. Maybe Luke *liked* me. His friends left and there was a distinctly awkward moment on the couch. I was so surprised by the realization that Luke liked me that I didn't really have time to think about whether or not I wanted anything to happen.

'How do we do this?' Luke smiled before leaning over to kiss me.

I was instantly shocked by how good it felt. I hadn't even been able to imagine kissing anyone other than Anthony. Now, without warning, I was cocooned in another man's arms. I felt safe and loved once more. I wasn't about to let that feeling go. The following week Luke cooked me dinner and we started dating. He was generous and kind, always protective of me. But I didn't feel any deep connection.

As soon as Anthony found out I was seeing Luke, he asked me to marry him in his boyish laid-back 'why don't we' kind of way. I looked at him, the man I still loved, his beautiful naive innocence, and I wished he had asked me three months earlier for I would have jumped at it then, but it was too late now. Deep inside, as much as I wanted to believe him, I knew it was no more than a knee-jerk reaction to seeing me with someone else. The trust had been broken.

Luke adored me. I knew there were differences. He didn't seem to have any passion for anything; I had all the drive, and I didn't like that. But I ignored them: the feeling of safety and warmth when he held me was like a drug, powerful enough to put everything else aside.

I told Luke I loved him because I knew it made him happy. Maybe I meant it, at least in that instant, or maybe it was just fear masquerading as love, for I could feel an insidious fungus travelling through my body, a creeping feeling of unease that I tried hard to ignore.

I finished my degree and Jo and Dad came out to Australia. Together we took a guided camping trip to Uluru. I got on well with our tour guide who, like me, had a love of hiking and canyoning. I couldn't be sure, but I thought that he liked me. Unlike Luke, he had interests: things he was passionate about, like photography and the outdoors.

When we returned to Sydney, I felt deflated on seeing Luke. I could no longer ignore our differences. On New Year's Eve, when I looked at him all I could think of was how much I still loved Anthony, and how different that love was.

I was about to turn thirty. Life wasn't the way that, as a kid, I'd thought it would be at thirty. I didn't have a job, I had only just finished studying, and I had no home. So much was uncertain, but there was one thing of which I was sure: I didn't want to be with Luke.

I broke up with him, and on my thirtieth birthday I shared one last kiss with Anthony. It confirmed what I already knew: that we no longer had what we'd once shared. But being alone was not an option I wanted to entertain either, so I sent a card to our tour guide, Jack, thanking him for the holiday and suggesting we meet up next time he was in Sydney.

We arranged to go walking in the Snowy Mountains. Meanwhile, Luke and I had fallen into a 'friends with benefits' arrangement. I hadn't been able to let go of him, just as I couldn't with Anthony. It was as if I was only defined by the love others held for me. Luke didn't like the idea of me going away with Jack, said that Jack had played the oldest trick in the book when he'd told me that he had forgotten his sleeping bag. I didn't particularly fancy Jack but I let the fantasy of a life spent hiking in the mountains take over. When he kissed me for the first time it felt like a lizard was sticking its tongue down my throat. *That's okay*, I thought. *I can teach him.*

One morning, when Jack was at my place, the doorbell rang. It was early and I couldn't think who it could be. When I opened the door, Luke was standing in front of me. He said he'd been walking and thought he'd drop by.

'Uh ... uh ... hi ... um ... Come in.' *Shit. Why did I say that?*

Luke didn't know that I was seeing Jack. When he walked into the living room to find Jack there, grinning like a Cheshire cat, Luke just glared. We had a cup of tea. I talked too much, about anything that sprang to mind. Luke wasn't angry, he never got angry. He was flat.

When he got up to leave, I showed him to the door and he looked at me.

'Thanks for telling me, Tara,' he said, deadpan. Then he walked away.

I felt like a five-year-old kid caught stealing sweets from the local shop. *You're a bitch*, I thought to myself. But then I reasoned that I hadn't really done anything wrong. We'd broken up, after all. I started getting good at kidding myself.

I went up to Darwin to see Jack, still searching for the 'fullness' that seemed to elude me. Jack said he was going to move to Sydney to be with me. I pictured our life in the mountains together, outdoors, peaceful.

Back in Sydney, Luke and I caught up for coffee. Despite everything that had happened, he still wanted to be my friend. When we got up to leave, he kissed me, igniting once more that fire of attraction, and I melted.

We were back at my place when the phone rang. I let it ring.

Please, God, don't let it be Jack.

Then I heard his voice come through the answer machine. I started to sweat. Luke and I pretended not to hear, but the sound seemed to fill the living room.

'Hi, T. It's Jack! I'm finally on my way to Sydney. Can't wait to see you! Look after yourself. Bye for now.'

I turned to Luke. 'Shall we have a glass of wine?'

I blindly, desperately, defended my behaviour to myself. Luke and I are just friends, I told myself. He knows about Jack.

Jack and I aren't really together because he isn't in Sydney yet. This is just a one-off. No big deal. Just like that, kidding myself morphed insidiously into outright lying. I could feel my brother's disappointed eyes boring into my soul as his very own sister fractured his dreams of pure hearts.

When Jack arrived I felt the familiar nausea almost instantly. Two days later, I broke up with him. He sat on my sofa and cried. The only feeling I had was one of guilt.

He looked at me through his tears. 'How can you do this? Why?'

'I'm sorry. I made a mistake.' That was all I had to give him.

I couldn't answer his question. I had no inkling then of what had brought us to this, no desire to take a peek inside myself, for I was too busy grasping for any band-aid I could in a vain attempt to stem the flow of blood from my haemorrhaging wound. Jack told me I was a nice girl but that I had issues I needed to sort out. *You're the one with the issues*, I thought, and I believed it. No matter that the counsellor I had seen with Anthony had kept probing at my past. I was fine.

I continued to bash my way through the bush blindly, heading vaguely for some unknown place, applying band-aids as I went, haunted by my brother's words, how I betrayed him.

God, how I dream of passions of pure hearts. I cannot speak of feelings so well. I have a terrible desire to speak only in truth and only with purity, but this desire is a branch of my egotism, my desperate poisoned desire to be different.

I got back together with Luke again, revelling briefly in the high of the reunion, until the incessant, nagging voice telling me that I did not love him could be ignored no longer. I didn't know then that band-aids can't fight fungus. Indeed the moisture they trap merely fuels its growth.

I lived in a continuous state of internal conflict; my behaviour was so incongruent with the values I held. It was as if I were holding a jousting match between my ego and my true self. It was just as Adam had said:

If I could but hold a frame of sweet honesty in my head, un-perpetrated by the thrusting delusions of egotism ... then I could enjoy bliss.

I could not hold the honesty, for to do that I would have to entertain the crippling pain of the past. Instead, I kept running, but the truth followed me, as did the pain. It hunted me down wherever I went; my constant predator. I tried to protect myself with denial, but denial is flimsy and invariably gives way, like a camouflaged trap on the forest floor.

The feeling of being safe in the arms of a man was like taking a hit of morphine. It took the pain away, almost instantly. For a few stolen moments, I could once more be that little girl, sitting on my mother's lap, feeling her arms around me ... cuddling me, loving me and protecting me. To feel even for a second safe in the arms of another, to have for just one moment what my mother had given me all those years ago, no matter what damage it inflicted on others, was my constant lure, the habit that I could not kick, and it fed the cancerous growth within my spirit.

Even as a teenager, my brother had sensed the essence of the malignancy within us both.

As for my 'great love' for Sarah, well I think it is more of a pursuit of an ideal, of an image, even the possibility of it having something to do with Mum has crossed my mind, but maybe that's nonsense as I fell madly for girls before she died and all that has happened is that with growing older, the 'passion' has become deeper. Why I say this is because when I think of Sarah, I think nothing of her face, her manner, herself, but just some blurred image and deep sadness as though torn away from some love.

The cancer that killed our mother had metastasized into our lives, the symptoms of which became evident through our relationships. Neither Adam nor I knew what we were searching for. He searched as a teenager. At thirty, my search had still not begun.

CHAPTER 21

I started my intern job as a physiotherapist at St Vincent's Hospital in Sydney. I had always hated hospitals. My first memory of them, when I was seven, was being in the emergency department at the Royal Free in London. Adam had hurt his arm. I didn't like the smell; it made me feel sick. The room had started to swirl, and I had fainted.

Now I walked into the intensive care unit at St Vincent's and my throat immediately tightened. I looked around me at the fragile bodies, seemingly violated by the very tubes and machines that kept them alive, hovering on the brink, between life and death. I saw ashen-faced family members staring pleadingly at their loved ones. I saw myself.

I started treating a French Polynesian lady who had been in intensive care for several months. She had an antibiotic-resistant bug so she was kept in isolation. She had a tracheotomy so she couldn't talk and she didn't speak much English. I felt desperately sorry for her. I watched as day after day a relentless string of doctors came and peered and prodded her. I was always nervous when I treated her, for her connection to life seemed so tenuous. I was terrified I might do something wrong.

I looked into her eyes and I recognized the fear in them. Perhaps it was our shared fear that connected us, for gradually she and I found our own language to communicate, a mixture of hand signals, mime, spoken and written words. It was my job to help her to exercise, and to cough so she could clear her lungs of mucous. Every day she would look at me so sadly, as if to say: 'I'm dying, I don't want to do this,' and I would look back: *I know. I don't want to do this to you either.* She knew I had to do my job, and she knew also that she would not survive.

We found a compromise of sorts. I would barter with her in our mime language.

'If you do *un, deux, trois, quatre, cinq, six* leg raises, then I won't speak French to you any more.'

She found my ridiculous attempts at speaking French amusing. She'd smile, as much as the tubes would allow, and that would give her enough energy to lift her leg off the bed, at which point I'd cheer as if she was running the last four hundred metres of the marathon in a forty-degree heat, which essentially she was. At other times, when she could no longer smile and encouragement seemed banal, I'd squeeze her hand and look in her eyes.

If I couldn't get her to cough hard enough I'd have to suction her, sticking a tube down her throat to suck out the gunk in her lungs, to prevent her from drowning in her own mucous. I hated doing it, watching the fear in her eyes as I took hold of the tube. She would blink to sign that she was ready. Some days she would refuse.

For me, the act held its own horrors. I always pictured the nurses suctioning my brother as I watched on helplessly as his body jolted from the unwanted invasion of his body.

On the days my patient refused to be suctioned I would continue to mime and scribble and talk, until eventually we might manage ten leg extensions. Then we'd both take a deep breath and smile, and I would write triumphantly in her notes: *10 × leg extensions: 2kg.*

I think she knew I was struggling with some issues of my own, something deeper. I'm sure she sensed my ferocious self-doubt, for one day she scribbled on a piece of paper: *You are very good.*

She died soon after that and it dawned on me that maybe, just maybe, while I may not have been able to 'save' her or even make a difference as a physiotherapist in the way I was supposed, I had made an impact on her life simply by connecting. But, as Adam said:

How dare I compliment myself, I am frightened to …

I thought of the picture on my living room wall, *The Art of Life*, the two lonely souls in hot-air balloons, and the line linking the balloons to each other. Perhaps connection formed the essence of life. If I had been able to connect with Adam, would he have died?

Soon after, I had a hauntingly intense dream.

My brother and I are walking together down a long dusty road in India, a few dishevelled shacks on the side of the road and a couple of lonely figures shrouded in saris, only their silhouettes visible in the fading light of dusk. They are standing, watching; present but aloof. I cannot see their faces. Adam leans heavily on me. He is ill, painfully ill. He cannot stand properly. He cannot walk. There is an urgency to move forward yet I begin to buckle under his weight, trying to support him as his legs give way beneath him, like a rag doll. 'We must move forward,' I urge him, but his weight is too great for me. I look ahead of me at the long road as it disappears in a haze of dust on the horizon. 'Please help … Someone help us …Help!' I call but no sound comes from my mouth for my throat has a vice around it. I feel a deep entombing pressure, a gnawing, suffocating heaviness. Panic rises within me. The figures on the roadside remain still, watching, silent, my own voice mute as I collapse under the pressure. No one helps. They only stand and watch as the earth swallows me and my brother slowly, and we sink into nothingness …

I awoke, paralysed with fear, sweating. I felt my brother's soul upon me.

Sorry, Ad. I couldn't help you. I couldn't save you.

That dream encapsulated perfectly so much of what lay unaddressed within my heart. Adam's death had left me with a seemingly unending feeling of failure. My love hadn't been

125

enough. I hadn't been able to save my brother or my mother. I couldn't even help my father. I had never felt guilt, only overwhelming helplessness and shame. The feelings drove me to rescue anyone I could, so that it wouldn't have all been in vain, except it was never enough. I was never enough.

I often looked at people in intensive care and wondered if they would ever get out. I had a patient in his late fifties who had been in the high dependency unit for months. He had a tracheotomy, and I couldn't see how he would ever get better; his body, along with his will to live, was wasting away before my eyes.

It was Christmas Day when I decided to take him outside to get some fresh air and see the sky. We hooked up the machinery, the tubes, the bags of solutions and the oxygen and wheeled him through the sliding doors of the hospital's front entrance, only to be greeted by a wind that carried with it the smoke and ash from the bushfires that were raging around Sydney in 2001. So much for fresh air, I thought as I watched him slump a little lower in his wheelchair, lapsing into semi-consciousness. I prayed that this wouldn't be the last breath of outside air he ever took. I didn't know then that those fires would soon be a part of my life.

Several years later, I was walking down the street near my home one morning, when I passed a middle-aged man. He looked familiar but I couldn't quite place him. Then I noticed the marks of a tracheotomy scar on his neck. I realized it was my patient, the picture of health, strolling along in the fresh spring air. It served as a reminder to me that, just as smoke and ash clear, so people can and do come back from hopelessness.

I thought of Adam. Could he have come back from his desolation?

I want to die now … Well, I don't really …

Then I think of other patients, the ones with traumatic brain injuries. The ones with whom I had found it impossible to connect. Incoherent and frustrated, they had been robbed not only of their social skills but also their personalities.

Barry was one of those. He'd throw his arms and head around in anger and frustration. One day I would be thinking that I had made a difference, only to find out on the next that he had forgotten everything I'd taught him. His family told me he'd been a fun-loving larrikin with a sparkling sense of humour before his motorbike accident.

Would I want that for Adam?

I recalled the nurse's words: 'Adam will never be the same if he survives this.'

I knew then that it was better that he had died than he had lived a life of dependency and anguish, no longer the beautiful person he had once been.

I arrived at work one morning to find the receptionist absent from her usual spot at the front desk.

'Where's Annie?' I asked a colleague.

Without answering, he handed me a letter written by Annie from her bed in a psychiatric hospital. She had just attempted suicide. With intense horror I read the words on the page in front of me as she struggled to explain her actions. I felt every word of her desolation, her guilt and her regret. I saw how the darkness had ever so slowly enveloped her, strangling her ability to see a way out. Her words reached into my soul, to the delicate part where Adam lay and grasped the hopelessness and the despair. I wanted to run, to get out. I headed straight to the bathroom, locking the door behind me, desperately trying to keep the dam in place that held behind it an ocean of tears. I had a list of patients to see, so I willed myself not to cry, squashing the tears back down until only a faint persistent trickle expelled itself as a glassy film across my eyes. I struggled through my day at work, desperate to get home. Compassion was calling me, screaming at me to reach out to her. Finally I sat down to write and the words streamed from within.

I know that you are in a dark place right now and there must appear to be no end in sight, but one of the endlessly beautiful things about life is that it is constantly changing. What you feel now will be different today, tomorrow, next week and next year. I promise you that. There will be dark places in the future but there will also be light. Take those moments of lightness, however fleeting, and cherish them. Take hold of them and store them somewhere close to your heart so you can touch them when you need them.

I know it may be impossible for you to realize the good things you have at the moment … but try, please try. You have a mother and a father who love you and will continue to love you despite any pain you may have caused them. When your mother hugs you, remember how that feels. Remember how, for that split second, you can forget your pain and feel safe and protected once again. Remember the warmth it brings to feel the sun on your face. Remember these simple things that bring joy. There will be one thing in every day that brings light … just look for it, write it down and hold it close.

You are getting help and admitting you have a problem. That is a forward step. It is honest and that too is something that brings just a glimpse of light, far better and stronger than to hide behind an addiction. It is the hardest and most painful of times that also give one the opportunity to learn the most. The choice to learn is a blessing that you will count one day in the future if you can just persevere for now and try to take some solace from the simplest of things … the smell of some flowers, the sparkle of the stars or the taste of your favourite food.

I know this may mean nothing to you at the moment, but please keep this and read it again whenever you feel able to. I am thinking of you.

Tara x

It came from a place deep within my heart, flowing directly through my fingers and onto the page in front of me: one person reaching out to another, the Art of Life. I hadn't been able to help my brother but I could use what I had learned to help someone else. In doing so, I took one more step toward healing myself.

CHAPTER 22

By now it was two years since I had first broken up with Luke, yet I was still embroiled in an on–off relationship with him, unable to cut the cord completely. I clung on to the remnants of what I had with him as if I were holding onto a tree branch that kept me clear of predators on the forest floor beneath.

In fact, I hadn't been able to let go entirely of any of my ex-boyfriends. So it had seemed perfectly natural to invite Luke, Anthony and Jack to my birthday barbecue. They are all my friends, I reasoned. Although why they remained so I hadn't the faintest idea.

On the day, I sweated through one awkward conversation after another. *Hmmm … this is a little uncomfortable*, I thought.

Note: Do not invite three ex-boyfriends to one's birthday ever again.

My sister, who was over from England, shook her head in disbelief. 'You've gotta sort it out, Ta.'

When I heard her words, I abruptly lost my grip on the branch I clung to. It was the moment I finally recognized that something was wrong. Jo had held a mirror to my face and said: 'Look.'

Then, as if to prove a point, something happened that forced me to do just that. As it does for any addict, the energy and motivation for change only came out of the deepest cavern, when the destruction of my addiction became so great that it overcame the pain involved in moving forward.

In the middle of the night, I woke to find that my body felt different. My breasts were tender and sore. A feeling of dread came over me. I knew instantly that I was pregnant. It was long before any test was going confirm this, but I knew.

Oh God, no, please no.

At thirty-two years old, I felt deeply ashamed and disgusted with myself. How could I possibly have let it come to this?

I waited.

Finally, when my period was late I went to the doctor. The test, as I knew it would be, was positive.

I told Luke. We talked. He'd always wanted kids. I knew some part of him was devastated that I wasn't jumping for joy. He loved me, yet we both knew our relationship was a mess.

What I had always thought would be an impossible decision to make turned out not to be. Instinctively I knew I should have a termination. If I knew that I didn't want to have a child with this man, then I had to admit to myself that I didn't love him. If I didn't love him, what was I doing with him? Luke and I never slept together again. I finally did what my sister had told me to do. I began to look.

Ahead, I could see only a towering, unconquerable mountain. When I turned to look behind me I could see the earth I had scrabbled through following my mother's death; the quicksand in which I'd flailed after Adam's suicide; the river rocks upon which I'd hauled myself to save myself from drowning; the trees I'd climbed to escape stalking predators. Here I was at last, tiny and insignificant, at the bottom of the mountain, contemplating the climb ahead. I thought of Adam and his journey through the Himalayas.

The gargantuan mountains tower in jagged defiance. Huge razor rocks form the snow-flecked summit that gradually recedes into the rounded green pastures of the lower slopes. The thinness of the air was noticeable as soon as we had climbed the first mounds. The summit stood before us as the going became even more difficult. We began to use all fours to ascend the tortuous slope with rasping breaths and acid limbs. Scattered snowfields drained energy out of the soles of one's feet with sapping incessancy and soon the thinness of the air rasped at our chests. The great rock faces, knobbled and cracked, hemmed us in, diminishing us to appear as ants crawling through a castle.

Adam's words formed the perfect reflection of my internal landscape.

The realization dawned on me that I needed help to navigate the mountain for me and for my brother.

A good friend gave me the number for a psychologist. With a great deal of resistance and trepidation I made an appointment. My body quivered as I walked into Hannah's office. I felt as wobbly and vulnerable as a newborn calf. She directed me to a comfy chair and I sat down. There was something approachable about her; maybe it was the bobbed hair and freckles. She was a quirky woman, in her late forties, with an equally quirky dress sense.

'So …' she said.

Almost before she'd got the word out I dissolved into tears. Then, for the first time, I spoke of what had happened and I touched the pain.

Whenever I had spoken of my family history in the past, I would always hear myself say that my mother had died and that I did have a brother but that he had also died. I never mentioned my father's illness. I said the words but I was detached from them. I never felt any part of the story they told.

This time, as I spoke I connected with the words and the pain. It was as if I was having my first dose of chemotherapy; I felt nauseous but I was, at last, fighting the cancer within me. I had found the malignant tumour that was strangling my soul.

'What do you feel, Tara? Not what you think, but what you *feel*?' Hannah asked.

'I … I … don't know,' I stumbled, confused, just as Adam had struggled with the same question.

Why is it so hard to understand what you feel? Feeling is, in essence what your thoughts are, aren't they?

Week after week I went to see Hannah as she helped me understand this very question, to find the essence of my feelings. Ever so slowly, I began to realize that thoughts contaminate feelings, hijacking their purity. Adam had felt this too.

This mind and heart of mine will not let pure feeling through.

I couldn't be honest because I didn't know what I felt, only what I thought. It was just as Adam had said:

All good and honest feelings that I have are imparted with double thoughts – those just recognizable suspicions that stem from nowhere and are beckoned by no part of the consciousness but humiliate your mind with their falseness.

My brother and I grappled with the same confusion. I began to realize that to touch the feeling, not to think it, is to find the truth behind the tears. When I stripped away my thoughts, which I had so carefully but unknowingly sculpted to protect me, what I found was an overriding feeling of fear: fear of being alone, fear of darkness, fear of heights, fear of failure, fear of the past and of the future. Fear pervaded almost everything I did and felt. To reach the essence of my fear, I knew I had to retrace my life, back to childhood, and identify where it came from. I had shed a million tears before I met Hannah but I had never connected with what lay behind the emotion. I had never truly *felt* it.

One by one I had to walk out into my fears, stripping back the layers. Therapy opened the door for me, but I had to do the work. I had to 'live' the changes, learn how to look at things in a different way.

I began to realize that I used my relationships to shield me from my fear of being alone, just as Adam had.

Sarah was as sweet as ever and it made me feel free from all my ...
I don't know what you call it, maybe loneliness – yeah, that's right.

As it has a habit of doing, the universe conspired to put me in a position where I could choose to face my fears. I had been looking to buy a two-bedroom unit, but I kept missing out. I was about to give up, convinced I couldn't afford anything, when I fell in love with a one-bedroom unit that sat on a roundabout and had water dripping through the kitchen ceiling. I made an offer on the spot and, just like that, I was forced to spend time alone. I kept busy, almost as if I was frightened to stop, for if I stopped, I might have to think, and I didn't want to think. I didn't want to look inside. Adam had, and it had killed him.

Ever so slowly, almost imperceptibly, I learned how to be alone, how to sit with myself in the light, and then in the darkness. I slowed my pace from a sprint to a jog. I began to realize that if I started thinking about things, I could stop if I wanted. I could take a peek at my past without unleashing the unstoppable torrent of pain that I had experienced before. It didn't mean I would become engulfed by it as Adam had.

I looked on it as a training programme. If you want to run a marathon, you must build up slowly or you will become injured. You alternate between walking and jogging, increasing the amount of time you run, before you can go the distance. I trained myself to be alone in a similar way, spending the odd evening at home on my own.

I was vulnerable during the nights. I hated the darkness, the way it enveloped and trapped me. Danger is at its greatest at night: you cannot run in the dark. In the dead of night I'd said goodbye to Mum and Adam had jumped from his window. I had to learn that sitting alone quietly in the dark is safe, and that I could face the fear. Then, perhaps, the beauty of silence could emerge.

Gradually, facilitated by Hannah, I stripped away the layers, as if I was a Russian doll. I searched for the smallest one, the inner child cocooned within all those outer shells of protection, still inaccessible.

Then, one day, about a year into therapy, I sat in her office and she gently probed me, steering me toward Mum. I had spoken endlessly about Adam and Dad, but up until now we had not talked a lot about Mum for I struggled with my memory. It felt blocked. There was so much I could not recall about that time. Then without warning I started to cry.

'I never cry about Mum,' I sobbed. It was strange, I seemed to cry so much, yet never about Mum.

'Well, it's about time you did,' Hannah said gently.

For twenty-odd years I had never grieved my mother's death. I hadn't felt the pain of losing her as I had felt on losing Adam. I clung on to her that day and every day since.

Slowly I started to piece together some of the lost time when Mum died. I went through every detail that I could remember. I retraced, step by step, the events of the weekend she died. I went through exactly what I had felt when I woke in the middle of the night desperate to see Mum.

Images came to me in fragments. There was something about floors in the hospital. Had Mum been moved? Perhaps they had moved her and maybe I had been to the hospital and been panicked when I couldn't find her. Had I thought that she had died distraught that I had not got there in time and that no one had told me? And I remembered the three of us sitting at Mum's bedside in a private room trying to say goodbye.

Then, as I remembered, so the nausea rolled in. It welled up inside me in surges, like the swell of the ocean, overpowering and tumultuous, squeezing the hurt, squeezing the pain, squeezing the grief; my chest, my stomach, my throat, all contracting, trying to purge themselves of something, as if drowning in salt water.

As I sobbed and wailed I felt within my body the warmth and safety of my mother's arms around me, and I felt the loss of her through my being.

Following that session, I watched the sadness emerge within me, just as Adam had.

If I could explain my own sadness, which perhaps I can if any consciousness would let me, then maybe I might be more vital, more worthy of life than I am. If I see with my eyes, then I am a self-pitying wretch, as no doubt anybody who may read this one day will undoubtedly conclude. I thought I had finished with it all, but obviously I cannot rid myself of this 'nausea'.

It was exactly as Adam had said. I could not rid myself of it. Perhaps my brother was right.

I feel as if sometimes I was born to be a sad person. For are there not characters in this world that are by nature sad as there are those that by nature are happy?

I wondered, was that me too? It felt that way. People close to me have often said that sometimes my eyes glaze over and I retreat to some distant, unreachable place, but the sadness sits so comfortably on my shoulders that I am often unaware of its presence: *Struck by a weeping sadness, a tear of confused emotion.*

A few weeks later, as I allowed myself to feel the sadness, I walked down to my home beach of Bronte. I sat down looking out at the water and let the memories and the pain surface. I remembered the crematorium, how I stood and watched my mother's coffin move along the conveyor belt into the fire. I noticed my grief as I sat quietly on the beach. I watched it in my body. At first it had been in my chest all those years ago. It had moved to my throat like a vice, then up to the root of my tongue.

135

It was no longer raging, but was still pervasive and stifling, as if I was breathing through a straw from a bottle with no air. I began writing to my mother.

Dear Mum,

I don't know where to start. There is so much I want to say. I don't know why I haven't written sooner. What happened? What happened to you and to us? Where did you go? Why did you go? I need your love; I need to talk to you. It feels like I'm losing you all over again, or maybe for the first time. Maybe I wasn't strong enough to grieve for you all those years ago.

I miss you, Mum. I miss you so much. I want to reach out for you. I still wish you were here to take all the pain away, to take the fear away, to make me feel safe.

I remember when I found out you were sick, so sick that you might die, and you came upstairs when I lay in bed crying and you comforted me and stroked my head and cuddled me. Then one day you weren't there any more and I remember lying in bed at night crying and there was no one. I remember realizing what it was like to be fully alone. I feel that now, the same feelings are here all these years later.

I'm scared, Mum, so scared, just like when I was thirteen or fourteen and I remember coming home to an empty house. It was quiet and dark and there was nothing. It frightens me, Mum. I'm scared of losing my mind, of being out of control like Dad or even Adam. I'm scared of the darkness and the quiet. I'm scared of being alone, of feeling detached. I'm frightened of letting go, of having nothing left, of having no identity, of losing you and in losing you, losing myself also. I'm frightened of finding nothing. I want to be in your arms. I want to be safe. I want to feel your strength, to carry it with me. I want you to be with me still in my heart.

I hope that you and Adam are together now, comforting each other, looking down on me and Jo. I hope you forgive me, Mum, for all the times I let you down, for not being able to save Adam. I'm sorry.

I love you, Mum.

I stared out at the ocean, quietening my mind until it came to settle on the image of myself in the crematorium, my stifled scream. Where had it gone? Was that the reason for the tension I felt across my throat?

This time as I relived the memory, I rescripted it as I went. I wrote the script how I wanted it to be. I saw that same scene in the crematorium, except this time I was on my own. I knelt before the coffin and laid one hand on it and one on my heart, and I said goodbye to my mother, in my own time and with total presence, in the way that I had wanted it to be. Then I turned to myself, the thirteen-year-old girl, and I supported her, held her tight in my arms and whispered to her, *Everything will be okay, you will be all right, I will be here for you.*

As I wandered home along Bronte beach, lost in my sadness, a little girl came running up to me, interrupting my reverie. She reached out and pressed a single flower into my hand.

'Everything is going to be okay,' she said simply and she smiled at me with an angel-like purity. Then she ran away. I was dumbfounded. Bewildered, I stared at the single wild flower that sat in my hand. When I looked up, her father caught my eye and smiled at me. 'It's just something nice we like to do, to make someone happy.'

That little girl could never have known the impact she had on me, that day. In that fleeting moment she touched my soul; she gave me hope.

Therapy gave me tools and helped me to understand how they worked, so that I could bash a path through the thicket of my sadness. Therapy opened the door of awareness. I was no longer running blindly but had slowed to a walk, which had enabled me to look around at the beauty and the pain. Gradually I began to emerge, and again glimpsed the mountain ahead. I began to ascend once more, occasionally stopping to plan my climb, but often forgetting, in my haste, to look behind to see how far I had come.

CHAPTER 23

Hannah once said to me, 'Therapy comes in many forms, Tara.' I had smiled at the time, a little confused. For years while living in Bondi I walked tentatively past North Bondi Surf Lifesaving Club, wondering if people like me could go in. It always felt intimidating, bustling and busy, full of bronzed fit bodies carrying surf craft and rescue gear in and out of the club, proudly wearing their red-and-yellow patrol uniforms. It took me eight years before I finally found the courage to walk into the club and enrol in the bronze medallion course, driven in part by the memory of my mother's dying words to Adam: *Always remember that whatever you do, you are part of the community, the wider world, and every citizen has a responsibility toward that community, to care, to give and to take a share in responsibility for it.*

I became a volunteer surf lifesaver and almost by accident I was introduced to the sport of surfboat rowing, where four rowers power through the surf directed by the sweep standing at the back – the captain and the eyes of the boat. The sport is a part of lifesaving by virtue of the fact that prior to the advent of motorized craft the boats were used to rescue people.

I had never rowed in my life as became evident when I first got in a surfboat and promptly sat facing the wrong direction. The episode with my dad attempting to push-start the car by rocking it side to side did spring to mind.

After that initial mishap I discovered that surfboat rowing was indeed a type of therapy for me. It brought me far more than I could ever have imagined on that first day when I stepped in a boat at Botany Bay.

After I learned the basics of the sport in the flat water it was time to venture out into the surf. We had planned to go out on a day when the ocean was calm. Unfortunately when we turned up at Maroubra beach, the swell had other ideas. It suddenly looked bigger and angrier than it ever had before, but I felt a tingle of nervous excitement course through my body. We walked the boat into the water, jumping in quickly as the waves crashed around us, tossing the two-hundred-kilo boat around as if it were a feather. Once on the water, we found ourselves engaged in a wrestle with the ocean, smacked and jostled around by the waves. My fear dissipated, dissolving into the ocean, replaced by an overriding sense of joy. I squealed and laughed in a way I never had as a child. It was liberating, like the rafting on the Zambezi. There is something almost spiritual about finding that unison between your body, your sport and nature. Back on the beach I found myself throwing cartwheels, carefree and joyous. I had found my passion, and with passion comes clarity and connection.

We started training together as a crew. Rowing, unlike athletics, is all about the team. It's about timing, about doing everything together. We went to ridiculous extremes to ensure we were in time with each other, even training in the gym to a metronome. We built a team and being part of that team gave me an incredible sense of belonging. It was almost as if I had another family, for surfboat rowing can be dangerous. You have to look out for your crew. If the boat capsizes, the first thing you do is 'count heads', making sure your crew are all safe. You train together eight or nine times a week, seeing each other at your absolute worst and your absolute best and everything in between. It binds you to each other.

We started to compete. I hadn't competed in sport since my teenage days as a long jumper when my coach despaired of me for I loved training, but I hated competing. I was always one of those athletes that 'should have done better'. As my current coach says, racing is ninety per cent mental and ten per cent physical. I had all the physical attributes but my mind betrayed me. When I lost a race it merely proved what I already knew, that I wasn't as good as everyone thought I was. Really I was a fraud, just as Adam believed he was when he had written; *I have lied all my life ...*

In many ways I found the challenges of surfboat rowing to be a metaphor for life. When the ocean is flat and calm, the race is simple, the obstacles small, but so then the excitement and the opportunities for learning are diminished. When the surf picks up and the ocean is rough, the stakes are higher, the risks greater, the obstacles bigger, the highs are higher, the falls larger, but the joy, as well as the fear, is magnified. And so are the lessons learned.

I always went into races driven by the fear of losing rather than the desire to win. Not exactly the psychological attributes of a top athlete. I kept thinking that if I could just win this medal or that medal then I'd be good enough, but I never was. Then one day at the NSW state surf lifesaving titles something shifted. We had made the final and I walked toward the boat carrying my oar, nothing between me and the sun and the breeze and the water but a swimming costume. In that instant I was completely myself, one hundred per cent in my own skin, grounded in the present. I stood on the beach, staring at the ocean, waiting for our race to be called. The ocean was rough but a sense of calm prevailed within me. I knew all I had to do was my best. That was good enough, no matter the outcome. My heart and my body and my mind seemed to merge into one. In that instant the struggle dissolved.

The race was almost effortless, surreal. I felt a graceful power surge through my oar into my body as the boat sliced through the water. I saw a beautiful green wave building behind us, feeling its force build beneath us. With one powerful stroke, we pulled the nose of the boat over the lip of the wave and felt it take off, accelerating and scudding through the water, breathing life into my soul, the very essence of passion. We came home with a silver medal that day. It is one of the proudest medals I have ever won, for it was the day that I realized I didn't have to be perfect. I could let go of the curse of perfectionism that had hounded my brother: *I wasn't perfect and I couldn't accept it.*

In rowing we talk of inches. With every stroke you might only gain an inch on the crew in front of you, so that you don't notice the ground you're making until suddenly you've gained a boat length. So it is with healing. It comes in inches. Grief comes in waves; healing comes in inches.

PART THREE

Making Peace with the Past

CHAPTER 24

I decided that it was time for me to visit India with my dad. I had been on my own for several years now, building my confidence and my strength. Now was the time to take another step into my past. It had been over seventy years since my father had left his home country as a six-year-old. In all those years he had never been back. He had last seen his brother Shambhuji in London in 1970. They knew nothing of each other's lives. I needed to trace my roots and give my father the opportunity to trace his.

I looked out of the aeroplane window at the clouds below, aware of the tension in my body, the tightness in my stomach. Adam had loved India passionately but he had also become depressed while he was there. Had going to India been a catalyst for his suicide? Would it be the same for me? Was I strong enough? Would the emotional stress on my father be too great? Might it spark another manic episode?

I knew that this trip was about facing fears – mine and my father's. We were heading off on a journey laden with meaning and emotion.

I had flown to England so I could travel with my father. Now I glanced at him, at his soft chubby fingers as he fumbled with the finicky aeroplane food. His hands trembled as he battled with a yoghurt container that seemed intent on frustrating him. His anxiety was rubbing off on me.

Would he have anything in common with his brother? How would he cope with the poverty? Adam had died only two months after returning from India ...

'Oh, uh ... Tara.' I was woken from my reverie by my father's voice.

'Yes, Dad.'

'I need to use the bathroom.'

'Okay, Dad. Here, give me your tray. I'll come with you.'

I watched him tremble as he tried to undo the seat belt.

'I'll get it for you, Dad.'

Finally, after some kerfuffle, he was safely up and standing in the aisle, only to find there was a queue.

'Oh dear.'

'What is it?'

'Oh, oh dear ... uh, uh ... I think it's too late.'

I looked down to see a dark shadow track its way down my father's beige trousers. My mind flicked back to that morning, and the sight of his open suitcase. I remembered seeing only some absorbent pants, a couple of books, a razor, a toothbrush, and a pair of pyjamas. Nothing else.

At that moment, I realized just how hard this trip was going to be. My father was an old man and he was frightened. He had nearly pulled out of the trip altogether a couple of months before. I had promised I would look after him.

He had vivid images of the India he knew as a young boy: the village in which he had spent the first six years of his life; the house in which he had been born; his mother; sacred memories. I was worried they would be tarnished when Dad discovered that the place no longer looked the same as that tiny village in northern India that he remembered. I wanted to give my father peace, for I saw his torment and it devastated me to see him live it.

I had brought Adam's diaries with me, knowing that in many ways this journey was a pilgrimage in his memory, something I needed to do for my brother and for myself. I smiled as I recalled his first impressions of India.

In India at last! What an incredible place it is. I think perhaps one aspect of India worth noting is how totally unfrightening a place it is. Obviously, at first, initial bewilderment causes slight anxiety, but this rapidly evaporates, leaving only curiosity and delight. I feel so comfortable here, so unafraid of encountering new people and places. One also develops from this confidence a greater willingness to be independent and a greater desire to investigate further. People do not intimidate you but show you friendship and respect.

One becomes so submerged in the transient abstraction of India that there develops an unconscious acceptance of life and its miseries in your mind far deeper and broader than you would have ever previously imagined. Everything finds its place, just as the colour and the beauty do, so does the pain. But that is not to say one loses reactions to it all, they still pervade your general existence – the surprise, the bewilderment and the disgust. Yet somehow they are less raw, borne with a greater and growing assuredness, their edges refined and melted into one, sitting with a comfortable wholeness inside your head.

I hoped this trip would allow me to be at peace with the past at last, so that I would be able to sit comfortably with it, to respect and appreciate it for what it gave me, rather than suffering for what it had taken from me.

I had never met my uncle Shambhuji. After he had returned to India at the age of nine, he and my father had been worlds apart. Their lives, their education, could not have been more different. Shambhuji had had very little formal schooling; at the age of twenty he had been commissioned into the infantry, where he'd served for twenty-nine years, fighting battles in Pakistan and Kashmir. My father had two university degrees and a PhD.

Apart from Christmas cards sent every year they'd had no contact.

I wondered what my uncle would think of me, in my thirties, unmarried and without children, a woman who rowed surfboats. I was the antithesis of a typical Indian woman. I had been reassured by the email he had sent in response to my letter. He sounded like the opposite of my father; he wrote with passion about his life, and his love of the army.

At the arrivals hall at Mumbai airport we walked into a sea of Indian faces. I cast around to find one that resembled the photo Adam had taken of my uncle twenty years before, but one face seemed to melt into another. *Where are you, Uncle? Where are you?* No one came forward to claim us, the rejects, the last pick on the school soccer team. Only the taxi drivers seemed keen to adopt us.

'It's okay, Dad. Don't worry. I'll find a phone and call Aunty Urmila.'

Dad shrank into himself, cowering, as more and more people crowded around us, fascinated.

Finally, I managed to get through to the house in Pune. To my relief, my aunt answered.

'You are here, no?' I loved that Indian habit of putting a negative at the end of a question.

'Yes, but we can't find Uncle.'

She tutted. 'Oh, dear girl, Uncle has borrowed a mobile phone. You must call him.'

I dialled the number she gave and it rang for an eternity. Finally I heard a voice.

'Allo.'

'Hello, Uncle. It's Tara.'

'Oh dear, we must have missed each other!' my uncle replied in a beautiful, slightly staccato, Indian accent. 'What do you look like?' He giggled.

Like we walked straight out of a comedy show, I felt like saying.

'I'm big with dark curly hair …'

'Ah, yes yes …'

I saw a spritely and lithe-looking man strolling toward us with a broad smile on his face. *Was this him?* My father merely stood bewildered. Then the man reached out his hand to Dad with a tear in his eye, and I watched as the brothers' hands met for the first time in nearly four decades.

Dad's face lit up. 'Ah, Shambhu!'

My uncle ushered us off to a waiting car, chuckling all the while. He explained how he had felt something 'tickling his thigh' but that he had not realized that it was his mobile phone ringing until a gentleman standing next to him had alerted him to the fact. It turned out that he had not received the photos I had sent him so he'd had no idea what I looked like.

I felt instantly at ease with my uncle, and thought how accurate Adam's description of him had been:

Yesterday Shambhu and I visited Bombay. It was lovely to be with him. My uncle, what a human he is. He was as teasing and relentless as ever. You should have seen him playing monsters with the kids, the little girl a wide-eyed princess and the boy a naughty little monkey. How playful Shambhu is. He has that endearing sense of mischief. He is so human, so full of life and so different from Dad and Samarth.

Shambhu did indeed have a lovely cheekiness about him that almost seemed at odds with his military background.

On our first night in India I searched through my luggage to find the album of old family photographs I had put together at Shambhu's request. I had struggled to find any photographs of the five of us together. When I handed the album to him I felt the warmth and joy and sadness in his heart as he carefully turned each page, piecing together the last four decades.

'You know, Shambhu, I think it was wrong of our father to make you come back to India as a child.'

I heard the familiar rumbling anger in my father's voice.

'Ah no. No, Shivaji. It was my choice. Father never made me.'

'That's rubbish, Shambhu. You were a child. You had to face so much hardship.'

One of the many demons Dad carried with him was his guilt that Shambhu had grown up in India in a substantially less privileged environment than himself and Samarth in England. He had thought that by talking with Shambhu he might absolve himself of some of this guilt.

'No no, Shivaji, you are very wrong. Yes, it is true, for the first six months when I returned to India I found it very difficult.' My uncle chuckled as he recalled how he had not known how the toilet worked, could not understand the language, and how his uncle always pocketed the money that his father sent to support him.

'Yes, Uncle was a crook, but he meant well.' Shambhuji laughed and nodded his head; Dad tutted and shook his.

'You didn't have an education.'

'Ah, but Shivaji, I wanted to join the army. I'd always wanted that. It was not just our father's wish, it was mine too.' Then the tears welled in his eyes. 'You know, just the thought of Kashmir. Huddling together with my men under one blanket at fourteen thousand feet and walking out in front of them on the battlefield as they followed me ...'

'Oh dear, oh dear.' I heard my dad mumble under his breath.

Can't you feel the passion, Dad? I could connect so easily with what my uncle was saying. I recalled my time in Zimbabwe, and the feeling of belonging that came with rowing; the shared struggle, the shared joys.

When my uncle spoke, it came from his heart.

'I have had a very good life and I have been lucky to have had a career of my choice and to have enjoyed it so thoroughly. I would never trade that.'

My father continued shaking his head.

I wanted to shout, *Because life really isn't about material things, Dad!* But I didn't. I merely sat and admired the insight my brother had had at just eighteen years of age:

Surely happiness in life comes from sharing it with others ... a binding of oneself to its essence ... what a Western product I am – to think of happiness in terms of affluence ... Happiness in its essence is sharing and caring or compassion.

Even in his seventies my father was unable to accept that a life in India, a life less abundant in material wealth, could bring happiness. It seemed like a terrible irony when I looked from one brother to the other: Shambhu's vitality, his upright stance, eyes ahead; my father stooped over, looking down. A man bound by regret and fear; his own son, with all his privileged upbringing, lost to suicide.

Shambhu possessed a fundamental belief that what is meant to be will be. He spoke of the profound effect a meeting with a disciple of Rishi had had on him. He recounted how the experience had washed away his cynicism, engendering in him a belief in destiny and spirituality.

'That's utter rubbish, Shambhu. You know, if it wasn't for Joanna and Tara I wouldn't care about anything, and if the world ended, it wouldn't matter, quite frankly.'

I was stunned by the bitterness in Dad's voice, and found the sadness that followed almost intolerable.

'The only wish I have is that when I die one of my daughters will be holding my hand,' my father said quietly.

The following day we sat in the car, jostled around by the uneven road that led to the village where my father had been born. I looked out of the window at the dusty road. I thought of Adam and his journey.

Everywhere, the yellow dried mud dust reflecting the hazy, hot rays of the sun, wooden shacks and red concrete walls. The air is so sweet and sickly. A blanket of moisture that cuddles itself around you in immotile smog. Fingering into your throat as you breathe and all the time it comes as if laden with the dirt and rotting of the streets themselves.

All of a sudden, my dream came flooding back to me with vivid brilliance. I knew instinctively this was it, the place of my dream. I had walked along this road, trying in vain to carry Adam's weight. And with that thought came the realization of how much India held for me. It was to be a vital place on my path.

Eventually we drove into Burhpur, the village of my father's birth, which had since been engulfed by the town of Fategah, six hours' drive north of Lucknow. The old family house, however, still remained, owned by relatives. As we entered the grounds, an old lady, the wife of one of my father's cousins, greeted us, bowing her head, crouching to kiss our feet. I cringed in a sea of cultural awkwardness, just as Adam had.

I do at times feel so alien to Indian life that it is difficult for me to cope. But then I have not been overly endowed with social skills. I find myself thanking everyone all the time and smiling. I am so unused to all this pampering.

Then I saw my father's face light up as he caught sight of the old front door.

'I remember hitting my head on that metal knob there,' he said softly, shaking his head gently, as if he couldn't believe he was actually here. His eyes became alive in a way I had rarely seen, as if they were opening to another part of his soul that had been tucked away, kept private.

My father and his brother walked around their old house slowly, stopping to relive the memories as they went.

'Ah yes, yes. I remember playing marbles over there.'

'And do you remember how we used to fly kites on the roof?'

Shambhu took his elder brother's hand to steady him as they ascended the steep spiral stairs.

'And this is the room you were born in, Shivaji.'

And there, in that room of his birth, we sat to drink tea and eat brightly coloured Indian sweets.

Finally we returned to Lucknow, to one of the many cousins' houses. It was a humble place, which they had turned upside down to accommodate my father and me, vacating their own beds for us. The small living room was dominated by what I can only describe as an aeroplane propeller which doubled as an air-conditioning unit.

Over the course of the evening relatives began to appear, some of them having travelled for days just to see us. Before long, the small living room was overflowing with immaculately dressed cousins, uncles and aunties. Many didn't speak English, but seemed happy just to come and look. When it got too hot, the propeller was switched on, creating such a racket that all conversation was drowned.

The women in their colourful saris fussed and pampered, urging us to eat, yet touching nothing themselves. My father didn't seem to be bothered that many of our visitors didn't speak English. He began to monologue incessantly, ranting about India and its socio-economic problems. Although Shambhu tried to tell him that the caste system was much less harsh than it had been, Dad motored on without listening, telling everybody how it should be changed. He made judgment after judgment about India, stating that everyone must want to get out of the country, completely unaware of how he was insulting the others in the room.

'That is utter rubbish, Shivaji,' my uncle would interject.

It was clear that everything Dad knew of India came from books he had read and from his own childhood memories of his birth country some seventy years before. His conversation bore no meaning to those around him. He did not hear or listen to anything anyone said, merely continuing on his relentless tirade, a turbulent sea of knowledge that ebbed and flowed, allowing no rational response, no human interaction. I looked at my father as he rocketed from one subject to the next, and I found him arrogant. I saw the madness in him.

I started to keep a tally of Dad's monologues as a way of keeping myself sane. I recorded the maximum time spent in continuous flow, without interruption: nine minutes, quite impressive. The number of monologues per day ranged from five to a seemingly infinite number. Occasionally, when I tried to curtail one with a gentle nudge or a look, Dad would say, 'I'm talking too much.' Then we would have a moment's respite before he motored on.

I watched Shambhu contemplate his brother. He tried to argue with him, telling him that he was talking all 'cock-eyed' but he could see Dad wasn't listening. Then, when Dad continued his monologue, his brother would say nothing or walk away. Shambhu would look at me as he did so, and his smile of empathy was worth a thousand words.

I tried valiantly to remain calm in the face of my father's madness. I breathed, I meditated, I wrote a journal, and I practised compassion ... until finally I lost my temper. I took Dad aside and screamed at him:

'Just be quiet! Be aware of the people around you, for Christ's sake. You're not listening to a word anyone says. You're judging people in their own country. It's embarrassing. Arrogant. They live here, Dad. It's their country!'

He responded as if he were a child: 'Fine, I won't say anything then.'

Then he sat quietly in the corner of the couch, eyes scrunched up, silent.

I felt guilty then. Was saying those things wrong of me? How should I have dealt with it? Was I merely projecting my own beliefs upon my father? Did I react out of my own fear that Dad's negativity would infect me? Did I want him to be quiet for my own sanity? Or was I just trying to protect others from my father, trying to save them from the discomfort of their embarrassment?

My father and I were two reacting elements, both vulnerable and frightened. Unknowingly, he pressed all the triggers within me that had been sensitized by my past. I realized that the anger I felt was telling me something, only I didn't yet know what it was.

'I'm sorry, Dad. I shouldn't have shouted at you.'

'That's okay, Tara.'

Then he went straight back to talking, as if I'd given him a leave pass.

'What happened to Adam?' my uncle asked as we sat in the car on our way back from visiting Philibit, the birthplace of my grandmother.

I glanced at my father. Until that moment, I had been unaware that Shambhu had never been told what had happened to Adam.

'Adam took his own life,' I said quietly. 'He'd been depressed for a while. It was hard for him after Mum died. He wasn't happy at Oxford and I think he found it very difficult to adjust after he came back from India.'

'That's rubbish, Tara,' my father interjected. 'It was those bloody deans at Oxford.'

'Dad, he was booked to see a counsellor the week he died.'

'It's so bloody corrupt. They should have seen. No one took responsibility for what they did. Why would Adam have done what he did? Why was Adam wearing some bogus Indian clothes when he came back from India?' Dad almost spat the words in his bitterness and rage.

I wanted to scream, *What about you, Dad? You were his father and you didn't see it coming ...* but I didn't. I couldn't do that to my father. Instead, I said this:

'You know, I have learned so much from everything that happened. Of course I wish he was still here, but maybe I wouldn't be the person I am if Adam hadn't died.'

'Don't be ridiculous, Tara. You can be so bloody naive.'

I felt a tightening sensation across my throat as the toxic negativity of my father's words swept over me, massacring my hope, the very meaning for life I had sought so hard to find. It was as if Dad was seeking to shred every bit of understanding and peace I'd found. Shambhu saw my hurt and when he spoke it was as if he was speaking my thoughts for me. He seemed instinctively to understand, validating me and helping me to hold some peace.

We took an overnight train from Lucknow to Agra to see the Taj Mahal. The train was several hours late and by the time we reached the Taj the sun was beating down. The journey, the emotion and the heat took their toll on Dad and he became faint and dizzy. I held him and we rested. As we sat, I pictured my brother sitting in the very same spot twenty years before, and before that, my mother in 1962.

I reached out to steady my father. He looked frail and vulnerable. *Is this all too much for him?* I helped him to his feet and we walked slowly toward the Taj Mahal. I watched his face brighten with wonder.

'Are you glad you came here, Dad?'

'Yes, yes, I am … I have learned so much,' he said softly.

'Do you still need to talk with Shambhu?'

'I still think my father was wrong to make him stay in India. I don't believe what Shambhu says. Why does his leg twitch when he talks to me?'

'Shambhu has told you. He was desperate to join the army. He loves India.'

Finally we travelled to Pune, where Shambhu and his wife Urmila lived. I recognized the house from Adam's photographs. Dad slept in the room where his son had slept. Adam had left his diary in that room – the diary I had with me now, which Urmila had passed to Jo when my sister had travelled to India.

Shambhuji took me for a ride on the back of his scooter. I couldn't stop laughing as we wove our way through the streets of Pune, smiling as I related to Adam's experience of Indian roads.

An Indian road is a very strange strip of land, used by innumerable conveyances and animal types. You are never quite sure what will happen on it next. Things tend to wander with scant regard for others, all the time sounding loudly their presence with those infernal horns. Put all this together with the hordes shouting in excited voices and the constant stream of tooting rickshaws, bicycles, scooters and trucks and the chaotic bombardment all your senses receive can be half imagined. In fact, the nasal information you encounter seems so far to be a good analogy of life in India. One minute you are enjoying the spicy aromas of food cooked on open fires or in clay ovens, and the next you are stifled by the stench of sewage.

Adam was so right: *India is chaos that works.*

My uncle introduced me to a young friend of his: 'This is my niece from Australia.'

'You are not looking alike,' the young man commented.

Shambhu smiled, 'Ah yes, so different in looks but in the heart, the same.' And he placed his hand on his heart and patted it gently.

Emotion overwhelmed me, the tears of twenty years welled in my eyes and in my heart. I had known my uncle for ten days and yet in that short time he had had the impact of a lifetime. So many times my uncle had said the words I would have said myself. We had grown up in different cultures, a generation apart; we had led such different lives, but we shared so much. I had never known if I was like my mother, and I know I do not think like my father, yet in my uncle I saw myself. I found the validation I had sought so hard to find in my father. I have no doubt that we were meant to come into each other's lives at this time. He touched my heart and I his, I knew this.

The day of our departure had come. We were running late, caught up in the chaotic Mumbai traffic. I started to get anxious that Dad might miss his plane. We were on different flights, his due to leave eight hours before mine. Shambhu wasn't allowed into the ticket hall without a ticket so he waited outside while Dad and I rushed toward the check-in area.

I started filling in departure forms frantically. 'Hurry, sir. Please hurry!'

It was then that I realized that Dad had not said goodbye to Shambhu. I knew that they would never see each other again and suddenly it seemed as if the whole trip would be meaningless if they didn't get to say their farewells.

I dragged Dad away from the check-in counter. Dad hobbled and limped behind me. I could hear the agitation in his voice. He needed to say goodbye.

At the airport doors a guard stepped in front of us.

'You cannot leave the airport, ma'am.'

'What do you mean?'

'Once you enter, and have shown your ticket, you cannot leave.'

'But my father needs to say goodbye to his brother!'

In desperation, I scanned the sea of Indian faces outside, looking for Shambhu, willing him to appear. *It cannot end like this*, I thought.

After what seemed like an eternity, I glimpsed my uncle's smiling face and there, in the chaos of passengers, doors, trolleys, luggage and security guards, the two brothers embraced. Seventy years of emotion in one short hug between two old men.

My mission was done. I had not been able to bring my father the peace that I had wanted for him. It dawned on me that one doesn't find peace in another person or a place or even an experience. I had to find my own peace from within; only then could I help Dad find his. Similarly, Shambhu hadn't been able to take away Dad's guilt, but I had faced my fears and I knew that I had helped Dad face some of his. That was the best I could hope for.

CHAPTER 25

I sat in my father's living room at his home in Norfolk.

'Uh, Tara ...'

'Yes, Dad.'

'I need to get some new shoes. These are really quite uncomfortable.'

'That's fine, Dad.'

I looked down at his feet. The entire back part of the shoe was crumpled under his heel and I had to bite my lip to stop myself from laughing.

'Um, Dad, you're supposed to put your heel *into* the shoe, not on top of it.'

'Ah, I see, I see.'

I watched my father dither, his increasingly diminishing frame dwarfed by the piles of books in his living room. He was wearing an old hat; his trendy cargo pants, bought for him by Jo, sat on his hips, lopsided, due to the twist in his spine from the tuberculosis that had ravaged him as a young man. His white goatee beard shone against his Indian skin, still silky even now.

'Ah ... yes, yes ...'

He talked to himself softly as he walked over to the washing machine holding the milk, only to realize at the last moment that it wasn't the right place for it.

'Ah yes, the milk must go in the fridge,' he muttered.

159

I would have laughed if it hadn't have been so sad. I went to the sink and began washing the dishes, scrubbing the thick layer of scum from the sides of the cups. I felt my father's presence over my shoulder, hovering.

'What are you doing, Dad?'

'Ah, I see ...'

'What do you see, Dad?' I questioned, trying to track the train of his thoughts.

'I'm just watching how you do that.'

He studied my hand intently as it scoured the cup.

'It's the washing-up, Dad. I'm washing up,' I said, bewildered.

I was stuck somewhere between the urge to fall on the floor with hysterical laughter and feeling a deep concern for his welfare. How much of Dad's behaviour been due to his illness, how much due to his own particular brand of eccentricity? I didn't know. The previous year he'd sent me a birthday card, only it was a Christmas card that Dad had adapted by crossing out the word Christmas and inserting 'Birthday' in its place. I had smiled when I'd received it. Classic Dad, I'd thought.

He had developed his own methods to help him negotiate his way through the world. He carried a little notepad everywhere he went, scribbling in it to remind himself to ring me in case he should forget. He even wrote down what questions he should ask: 1) How are you? 2) How is work? 3) How's your flat?

When we spoke, our phone conversations went something like this:

'How are you, Tara?'

'I'm good, Dad.'

'How is your ... um ... err ... personal life?'

'I'm still on my own, Dad, if that's what you mean?'

'Oh, oh dear ...'

Thanks, Dad, I feel so much better now.

'You can always adopt, you know?'

What? Where the hell did that one come from?

'It's not as easy as that, Dad, and anyway, I'm okay. I've got lots of good things in my life. I'm happy here.'

'Yes, but you're all alone.'

Thanks for pointing that out, Dad.

'I have really close friends that are always there for me.'

'Ah, but that's not the same, Tara. People always have others things. Their own families.'

'My friends are my family, Dad.'

'Don't be silly, Tara. People will always take advantage of you.'

Hmmm … Time to change tack.

'I'm lucky, Dad, I've got lots of good things in my life. I love my job—'

'Oh, you shouldn't work too hard.'

Okay, try again.

'I've been out to the pub with some friends.'

'Oh, you're not drinking too much, are you, Tara?'

By this point I wanted to explode. It was as if I wasn't allowed to be happy or optimistic. He could never just say, 'That's great, Tara. Well done.' Everything that I did, everything I had achieved and was proud of, he quashed with toxic negativity. To me his pessimism and regret felt like the silent contaminants contained within the smoke created by a fire. Once inhaled, quietly and insidiously morphing into a deadly cancer.

I thought back to a conversation I'd had with my father during his visit to Australia. We had been walking around the beautiful rolling red rock formations of Kata Tjuta where the land exudes a spiritual essence that makes you want to reach out and touch life. I wanted to connect with my father after all these years, to finally talk of Adam's death. I hoped that our two isolated bubbles might touch, just for a moment.

'You know Adam wanted it, Dad.'

I felt his body stiffen. 'That's rubbish. Somebody has to be held accountable.'

My father's voice simmered with suppressed rage, and I felt my own calmness dissolve.

'Adam chose to do that. It was his decision.'

'Done be ridiculous, Tara … All those people …' Now his whole body was quivering and his anger was frightening me.

'What people?'

'All those supposed friends. Just in it for themselves. They all wanted something.'

I felt a sudden need to vomit.

'Dad, they helped us. They all did. They loved Adam and they wanted to help.'

'Don't be so bloody naive.'

It was as if my father had dropped a chemical bomb on the beauty that surrounded us. How could he be so wrong? How could he blame the very people who had sustained us? How could he be so angry?

I had to tuck it all away again, pushing it down.

In the hours I sat with Hannah, we talked a lot about my father. Our relationship was one that I could still access, that could be changed. I knew I could not change him, but I might be able to change my reactions to him. And I needed to allow myself to have a voice, a chance to expel the cancerous toxins I'd ingested.

When I was ready, I sat down and wrote to him:

Dear Dad,

I have been wanting to write you a letter for some time now. I just feel that there are a lot of things that I would like to explain to you. Things that are important to me, that I want you to understand – as my dad.

First of all I want you to know that I love you, but often I feel that we don't understand each other as well as we could. More than anything, Dad, I want you to acknowledge and respect how hard it was for me when Adam died.

I know that your life has been hard and that you have suffered many losses and sadnesses. I can never truly know what your life has been like or feel the pain that you have felt, just as is true for you of me. By that token I am asking you to acknowledge and respect the losses that I have had.

At times I have tried to explain to you how it was for me as a teenager and after Adam died. Your response has been that it wasn't as hard as your life, or that I don't understand. I found this really hard, that you didn't seem to understand that I was in pain too. That's why I want to tell you, by this letter, how it was for me during that time.

After Mum died and when you were in hospital and unwell, Jo was off with Ben and then at university, Adam and I cared for each other, we understood and respected each other. He was a family to me and I was a family to him. Then he died, the person I loved most in the world, the person who cared for me and knew me like no one else, the person that filled a void after Mum died. And he chose to end his life.

I was alone, completely alone as a teenager, having lost so much of what I loved. It was really hard.

I can only imagine from those feelings how it was for you when Mum and Adam died.

I have worked very very hard to come to terms with Mum's and Adam's deaths and even with your illness.

To me, the biggest achievement of my life is to have come through all this, a normal, happy person, content with life and able to help others. I am proud of that.

I guess, Dad, I just want you to understand that when I try to talk to you about the past, what I really want is just for you to say, 'Well done, Tara, you survived a huge trauma and a lot of grief and came out without feeling full of regrets and still with the ability to love and care for other people.'

I don't want to take anything away from you and your experiences and I can only imagine the pain you must have endured. I wish I could ease that pain for you, Dad, take some of the sadness and regrets away. I guess all I can do is to let you know that I love you and that I am really happy in Australia.

I remember very clearly when I was deciding whether to come and live over here, you saying to me, 'Follow your heart.' You were right, Dad, even though I'm sure it was hard for you to see me go. I thank you so much for that, for helping me to make the best decision of my *life. This is my home – where I feel happy and comfortable and at peace with myself.*

I don't want this letter to make you sad, Dad, but rather to build some understanding between us as father and daughter, because I do miss you, Dad, and I still need your love.

Take good care of yourself, Dad. I look forward to spending some time with you and Jo at Xmas.
With love
Tara

Writing was a gift that Hannah showed me. When things are confused and my mind torments me, writing helps. When I am unable to convey what I want verbally, because emotion clouds any clarity, I can write, just as Adam did.

I feel I am writing again in my narrow fervoured way, it makes me quieten.

I didn't know what response I would get, but I had at least given myself a voice. A couple of weeks later, I received this letter from my father:

My dear Tara,
I got your letter today. I am glad you wrote to me. I'll try and explain why I wasn't able to help you and Adam after Mum died. Of course I love you and am proud of you. But when I was ill and in hospital I was unable to think and feel anything except my own worries and preoccupations.

The tranquillizers they gave me did help but they also blunted the feelings and attitudes that I had. That is part of the reason I was unable to perceive and respond to the hurt that you, Adam and Joanna were feeling.

There are other things too which I hope will explain the way I behaved. They have a lot to do with my upbringing, my past experience and very personal experiences which will be difficult for you and your generation to understand.

I will not try to make excuses but I was astonishingly ignorant of all sorts of things like how to study, get a job, meet and talk to a girlfriend and the sorts of attitudes and motives and ways of behaving that were appropriate to any given social situation I happened to be in.

My head was filled with all sorts of foolish and harmful ideas that bore little relationship to the world I lived in.

It was lucky for me that I met your mother and we got married. Maybe it wasn't as good for her. I don't know. If I knew what I know now I would have behaved in a better way to her and to you, to Adam and Joanna.

If you ever have any children you will understand that children will always matter more to their parents than parents can to their children, and this is right, it should be so.

Only now, in my seventies, do I begin to understand and in a way come to terms with my own childhood and the parts that my father and mother played in it. They had horrific lives because of the malice and spite of others and other external circumstances. It is only now I have begun to appreciate what they had to cope with.

In a way, the way I have written this letter reflects the inadequacies of my own upbringing and my personality. But one is what one is and I can no more escape the fact that I am your father or you that you are my daughter.

Try and be happy. Happiness does matter. One can't escape the past but one shouldn't brood on it or let it run the present or the future.

We all have regrets and one of mine is that I haven't been able to and won't be able to transmit to you and to Joanna and to those whom I may come to care for, some of the understanding (little though it is) of the way the world is and human beings are and how to live one's life in a better way. But I am glad that you are content and believe that Australia is your home and where you wish to be. So let's have a relaxed and pleasant Christmas.

Life has to be lived. One has to earn a living, get food and water, wash, sleep and look forward to the next day.

Lots of love
Your father

Though I have finished the letter by writing your father, I am your dad as well, but I belong to an older generation where intimate feelings were rarely expressed in certain situations or documents. This had both its downside and its upside. The downside was the depression of feelings; the upside, feelings when expressed meant more.

I was mesmerized by my father's words. Tears fell silently down my face. I had learned more about him in those two pages than I had in my whole life.

Letters changed my relationship with him. Through them, I came to realize that he had insight far beyond that for which I had ever given him credit. When we talked, I heard only the projections of his inner world and his pain. His words did not reflect what he felt for me. He did not believe I was not good enough. It was I who believed that.

My reactions, especially the feelings of self-doubt, were projections of my own wounds. Writing to each other gave us an avenue for connection which we could not attain verbally. I began to understand my father. I realized, too, that my pain was not his responsibility. He had enough pain of his own. My pain was my responsibility and mine alone.

CHAPTER 26

We often curb our instinct and this habit makes us lie, there can be no honesty in it. We have lost what we were born to do, to live and discover and question ... I know not what I would naturally follow or in what way my mind would naturally function.

I had asked myself the very questions that had been niggling Adam twenty years before: What is my instinct? What was I born to do? What was Adam's instinct and what was mine? They seemed entwined.

I loved physiotherapy but my need to 'fix' everyone had left me feeling drained. I had a thirst for adventure, for freedom. I thought of the computer program in Edinburgh and what it had divulged all those years ago: *Number 1: Fireman.*

Adam had never felt he had the chance to choose his path. I had that freedom and I would use it. I waited patiently for the New South Wales Fire Brigade to run a recruitment campaign.

Before I knew it, I had quit my job as a physiotherapist and found myself walking into the state training college of the NSW Fire Brigade (now known as Fire and Rescue NSW), a trembling wreck about to embark on a new life as a recruit firefighter. I found myself in a bizarre new paramilitary world. All instructors and seniors were to be addressed as 'Sir' or 'Ma'am'. Our uniform had to be immaculate: caps to be worn at all times when outside; hair had to sit below the line of the helmet but should not touch the collar, no bobby pins allowed; bags should be held in the left hand when crossing the courtyard.

I looked at my mass of thick curls and wondered how on earth I was going to restrain them. After much trial and error, I discovered that the only way I could secure my hair was to coil it up at each ear, Princess Leia style.

'Firefighter Laaaal!'

I heard the shout reverberate across the courtyard of the training college as my class of twenty recruits lined up for roll call. My heart sank. *What have I done this time?*

'Yes, sir.'

'Your hair, Lal.'

'Oh, sorry, sir.'

I reached up and tried to restrain a stray curl that had won the battle to free itself, bouncing around in an act of defiance as if it were laughing at me: *Ha ha, you can't catch me.*

It was week three at the training college, breathing apparatus week. This would involve navigating our way in the dark through a smoke-filled maze in a super-heated building. I stood outside the training tower, sweating already from the weight of the apparatus and the uniform, which, by its nature prevents body heat from escaping. I have hated confined spaces ever since I went potholing in Wales as a kid, where I'd had to crawl on my stomach in the darkness, jammed, with solid rock above and beneath. Or perhaps it was the memory of Adam's face as we buried him in the sand. Why am I doing this? I thought. What *was* I thinking?

'Firefighter Lal. You're next. You're going in!'

I heard the door slam behind me and I felt the darkness and heat envelop me. It was immediately disorientating. The sound of my breath in the mask was deafening. I felt around for my partner. *Never lose contact with your buddy.* I knew that.

We fumbled for an opening in the maze. There seemed to be blocks in every direction, as if we were trapped in a box, one metre square. I tried to contain the panic. We found an opening, knee high, somewhere in the chaos and lay down, scrambling on our stomachs, heading in an unknown direction, air cylinders clanging against the sides of the metal maze.

We were supposed to be doing a left-hand search and rescue. That meant we had to keep contact with the wall on our left at all times, making a map of the route in our heads as we went. When we needed to return to the exit, all we had to do was turn around and keep the wall on our right. That way we shouldn't get lost: simple. Except that in the darkness, if you happen to lose contact with the wall or your partner, you lose the connection; disorientation kicks in. For just an instant, my partner and I lost contact with each other.

I was lost. *Breathe*, I told myself. *Breathe*.

'You're under the whole bloody maze, Firefighter Lal.'

'Sorry, sir.'

I gasped through my mask, sucking in the compressed air from my cylinder.

'If you can't find your way out of here, how the hell are you going to find your way out of a fire? Congratulations. You've just killed yourself, your buddy and your victim.'

The heat closed in on me, sweat cascading from every pore in my body. I felt myself shrinking, the same feeling I'd had as a child. *Just stay upright*, I told myself as we inched our way out of the maze.

Even a small fire can create huge amounts of smoke. One garbage bin can fill room upon room with thick dark smog. It is the smoke, not the fire itself, that most often kills people. They become disorientated in the darkness, and they panic, before becoming overcome by the toxic fumes.

I took off my uniform, pouring the sweat out of my boots, and went home. Once inside my flat, I let self-doubt consume me. The exercise I'd just failed had given me proof of what I had always suspected: that I was not as strong as others believed me to be. I wasn't good enough. I had climbed mountains, run a marathon, jumped out of planes, completed degrees, won medals

169

for rowing. I had built a body full of muscle in my desperate chase for some self-worth, but self-doubt always caught me, a predator that stalked me relentlessly. It was only some time later that I realized that no achievement, no gold medal, could give me self-worth, for it comes from the inside and you can spend a lifetime searching for it.

A close friend counselled me through the night and I woke the next day with a dull sensation of defiance. *I can do this*, I thought. I wanted to stick two fingers up to my fear.

I dragged myself into the college. Once more, I was thrust into the hot cell, the suffocating heat, the disorientating darkness. I looked for someone to rescue. This time, my partner and I found our victim, a hefty seventy-five-kilo dummy, and we dragged and hauled it out of the maze.

At this point something shifted. The self-doubt remained, but I realized that if I could only conquer the physical fears, perhaps the emotional fears could be resolved in a similar way. I started to see that maybe my greatest challenges were actually my greatest gift, for they gave me an opportunity to grow and to discover.

After I finished college, I was posted to the main station in Sydney, the biggest and busiest in New South Wales. I was barely even in the door of the station when the bells went.

'You're on the Flyer,' another firefighter called out to me.

'Flyer one, Runner one, automatic fire alarm,' a voice announced as the piercing sound of the bells, which are in fact more like a siren than a bell, finally ceased.

'Just follow me,' the same firefighter shouted. 'I'm Stick, by the way.'

Before I knew it, I was sitting on the back of the truck, flying down George Street in central Sydney, lights and sirens on, watching the peak-hour traffic part before us, like the parting of the seas.

'Grab the high-rise kit and follow me,' Stick directed.

I did as I was told. I donned my breathing apparatus, hopped out of the truck and grabbed the high-rise kit, affectionately known as the 'goat bag' in the brigade. Very apt as I'm a Capricorn and have carried that twenty-kilo bag containing a hose and various other tools up countless sets of stairs over many years. Carrying the goat bag is the job of the junior man (or woman in my case). As it turned out, it was just a false alarm. A workman had set off a detector with the dust created by his power saw.

'It happens all the time,' Stick assured me.

So began my life as a firefighter. Right from the start the guys taught me, guided me and helped me.

One night, early in my career, the bells went in the fire station, jolting me out of sleep. I fumbled for my overpants, put on my shirt, pants and boots, clipped up my belt and made my way down the corridor to the nearest pole. As I slid down it, I became vaguely aware that something was amiss. Something just didn't feel right.

My feet hit the floor and I began to make my way across the engine bay just as my colleagues began to appear. Still vaguely aware that something was wrong, I turned to look behind me, only to see my queen-size yellow bedsheet dragging like a train from its anchor point in the back of my pants. I began frantically reeling it in as my fellow firefighters fell about laughing.

'Hey, Linus, you bring your blanky with you on the truck this time?'

'Yo there, Batgirl. Where's your parachute?'

I couldn't help laughing. I call it my Bridget Jones moment. That's the thing about the fire brigade. I always laugh. My life has become lighter. There is a genuineness about firefighters that is both refreshing and grounding.

After a year or so, I became a relieving firefighter, travelling around to different stations. I worked hard to gain respect, often suppressing my femininity in my desire to prove myself. One day my colleague challenged me to an arm-wrestle. Of course I resisted, certain that I'd be thrashed, but he persisted until eventually I gave in, reasoning that I had nothing to lose. The boys gathered around and we sat down in the mess room facing each other, elbows on the table, hands locked.

'Get set, take the strain … go!'

At first I thought he was toying with me as we held steady. Then, slowly, drawing on all my strength, I pressed his hand down on to the table. The guys cheered in astonishment. Normy, my opponent, looked baffled, adamant that our arms hadn't been at the right angle.

'Best of three,' he announced.

'Sure,' I said, starting to feel confident.

I beat him twice more, apologizing to him after every one.

'Sorry, but you did ask for it.'

The boys rolled around in laughter, high fiving each other before proceeding to crucify poor old Normy.

'So how does it feel to get beaten by a chick ten years older than you, eh?'

'Pump it up, Normy!'

I was merely thankful it wasn't me. To this day legend precedes him wherever he goes. 'Are you the guy beaten by that girl in the arm-wrestle?'

I laughed. I'd been battling all this time for respect and all I had to do was have an arm-wrestle. Smiling inwardly, I recalled my mother shaking her head at me as I accidentally yanked the door handle off my bedroom door. 'You just don't know your own strength, Tara,' she'd said. And I thanked Adam for all those arm-wrestles he'd got me to have as a teenager with his friends.

Although it might seem at odds with the job description, being a firefighter showed me how to laugh again, how to lighten up. I formed a bond with the men I worked with that was respectful and caring, uncomplicated by any sexual relationship. When you go into a burning building, you know you have to trust the person you're with completely. And if my crew gives me a hard time, I know, underneath it all, that they care. They're like a family to me. We eat together, we cook together and we see each other at our worst at three in the morning when all you want to do is sleep. And when we go into a fire, we protect each other. That binds you more than anything. I thought of my uncle in India, his passion as he described the battles he fought with his men, how his eyes welled with tears.

I had lost half of my family. Now I have a new one, and I treasure it.

CHAPTER 27

Suicide call, Darlinghurst, Sydney, 2009

I am standing on the incident ground, holding the hose, washing the blood down the street. I bend down to pick up the broken pair of glasses. I hold them in my hand and look up. I see my brother climb through his window. I see him plummet head-first to the ground. I sense the instant of regret. Then I feel the impact through my body as he lands.

I watch the crimson-stained water trickle into the drain, washing my brother's life with it as it goes, erasing it. Controlling my need to vomit, I finish the job and climb quietly back into the truck.

'Why would you do that?' my colleague says. 'You'd have to be pretty desperate.'

I stare out of the window and say nothing. If I speak, I will vomit. *I'm okay. I have to be strong.*

My mother's words come back to me: *Tara will need all of you. It's fine. I don't need anyone*, I tell myself.

Wearing the uniform is like putting on a shield. It is a wall that, until now, has kept my emotional self separate from the strong, confident Tara I think everyone expects me to be as a female firefighter.

We return to the station and I lock myself in my bear cave. I start to cry.

There is a knock at my door. One of the boys comes in, bearing tissues and chocolate. He sits with me and I find myself telling him my story. I begin to let my crew see a truer, more authentic version of myself, complete with vulnerability. They surprise me with their empathy, their boyish compassion.

All this time I had tried so hard to hide what I thought were my fallibilities, my signs of weakness. Now it struck me that the ability to show emotion with honesty forms the foundation of connection. The bond came through showing my vulnerability, not hiding it. I realized finally that was strength, not weakness.

The incident that afternoon stayed with me. I went home, still feeling an uncomfortable sense of unrest within me, a deep sadness. I went down to the beach and looked out at the ocean. I sat quietly in the sadness, observing its thick, stifling presence. I could see no path through it. I wanted to reach out, but I didn't know who to. Today was Adam's birthday. I found myself writing without conscious thought.

16 September 2009

Dear Adam,

Today you should have been turning forty-one. How I would have loved to share this day with you, to drink a glass of wine and make a toast together, to have a run together or a game of tennis or even just to annoy each other as we always used to. Remember that game we played where we would climb on each other's shoulders and one of us would hang from the cornice in the living room while the other would see how many times they could run back and forth before they had to pick the other up? Or remember the time you kicked that door and then had to limp around for weeks after?

You always protected me, you looked after me – I loved that. I am as sad now as I was twenty-one years ago when you died. The sadness never leaves. I can only carry those memories with me and imagine the person you would have been today. Would you have been married? Would you have kids? What would you be doing and where would you be living? I know you would have led an amazing life, a caring life. You would have made a difference to people's lives.

Even now, even without life, you still do. I wish you knew that. Only yesterday I received an email from an old school friend whom I haven't seen in many years wanting to include you as part of a living tribute art project in Trafalgar Square. I declined; I didn't think you would want that. Was I right? Would you have wanted to be remembered publicly in Trafalgar Square? I think not, but perhaps it was my own selfishness that said no. To me you are mine. What we shared is ours. You are not a statistic, you are my brother, and I alone understand why you did what you did, or at least that's how it feels, and that is what I cling to – that intimacy and closeness to you. Something that is so starkly clear that I lack in my life, something that I yearn for.

I guess I protect you in your death as fiercely and tenderly as you protected me in your life.

Cheers to you, my gorgeous brother, on your forty-first birthday. I love you now as I always did.

Your big little sister x

There is no clean and tidy end to grief. It is not like a cut that heals when new skin grows, leaving no trace. Grief has a rhythm, abating at times when other things hold your attention, but always reappearing. It is like a mountain range undulating and unfolding before you as you navigate a path along it.

CHAPTER 28

'You're not giving relationship advice again are you, Bear?'
We were in the mess room at the station. Boaty rolled his eyes
affectionately, having heard the tail end of my conversation with
Big Gez. I laughed. I'd been doing what I liked to think I did
best: solving the boys' relationship woes. This, of course was an
on-going joke, given that I was the only person on shift to *not*
have had a relationship at all in many years.

'You've got this wall, T, this *wall* around you!' Big Gez
commented.

'Just protecting myself from you lot,' I replied, smiling.

I never chose men. I let them come to me. There seemed to
be less risk of rejection that way. With my wall, I was safe. If I
didn't let anyone get close I wouldn't have to risk losing them.
Unfortunately, there's always one who finds the fault line, that
one pivotal line that, once dissolved, causes the wall to come
tumbling down.

As I said, I'd been on my own for a long time. I felt quite happy
in my solitude. I had started to think about my brother's diaries
again, about writing a book. My instinct told me it wasn't my
time to meet anyone. But my friends were always on the lookout
for possible matches for me. If they happened to meet any
potential man they'd always bring up my name in a shameless
act of promotion on my behalf.

177

As it turned out, Rob had seen me at a surf-rowing carnival and wanted to meet me. I, of course had no idea who he was. My wall seemed inadvertently to stop me from 'seeing' anyone. My friend engineered a meeting in a busy pub and I got to take a sneak-peek, flattered that he'd noticed me. Rob was tall and fit with pale skin, mousey brown hair and smallish brown eyes that seemed a little too close together. He had a rugged rugby face that looked like it had taken a few hits, and he had a cute dimple on his right cheek. He wasn't gorgeous but he was nice-looking. I'm not sure who was more nervous – me or him. Habitually, I worried about appearing too keen with men, convinced on some unconscious level that I wasn't worthy of their attention, worried they would reject me.

Eventually, after a few nudges from my well-meaning friend, I plucked up the courage to go and talk to him. He smiled tentatively at me.

'Were you feeling the pressure like I was feeling the pressure?' he said, and that broke the ice.

He got my phone number from our mutual friend and we met up for coffee. He seemed like a nice guy and soon enough we started talking on the phone until he asked me out for dinner. Neither of us had realized it happened to be Valentine's Day. No pressure. He picked me up from home, shyly giving me a small red chocolate heart. I blushed and smiled.

'Thank you.'

'There's a place in Coogee I know. I hope that's okay.'

I was relieved. I knew the restaurant. It was casual, BYO and overlooking the water – just my type of place, nothing showy.

He showed me to his car, opening the passenger door to a shiny, sleek, royal blue Holden SV Ute, a kind of souped-up utility truck, which looks great but doesn't do a lot of hard work. It was distinctly fancier than my beaten-up old Toyota Corolla, not to mention twice its size. We arrived at the restaurant, which unsurprisingly was full of couples. I felt nervous, but as we sat opposite each other and talked, the apprehension melted. He told me about his career as a professional rugby player. We talked of the psychology of sport. I was fascinated. He seemed so humble of his achievements. It was as if he felt he wasn't worthy. He was almost apologetic as he described how he only played first grade 'off the bench'. I merely marvelled that he had a career as a sportsman. It had been something I'd only ever dreamed of as a child, when I'd imagined winning an Olympic gold medal even though I had no idea what sport it was going to be for.

I looked at Rob as I sat opposite him. I found his shyness endearing. Time disappeared. Before long, I looked up and everyone else had left.

When he dropped me off at home, I wondered what to do. Should I kiss him? Would he kiss me? He walked me to my door. Awkwardness prevailed.

'You know you can kiss me if you like?' I said shyly but with an uncharacteristic boldness.

'Oh,' he said and leant forward, planting a nervous kiss on my lips. We smiled at each other, not quite knowing what to do or say. Before he left we agreed not to rush things. I was adamant I wouldn't dive into anything.

Just as I climbed into bed he sent me a text message.

'Thank you for a beautiful night x'

I went to bed smiling.

After that he started sending me messages every day, telling me how beautiful I was and how lucky he was to have found me, how he didn't deserve someone as special as me. I couldn't understand that. He was the one with the successful sporting career, a lovely home and a great business. I didn't think I was special, but after a while his messages started to make me *feel* special. Every morning I would look forward to my phone beeping at me.

Gradually his words became like a drug to me; the more he gave me the more I wanted. He didn't let me down. The messages kept coming. Every day I was greeted by a string of poetic words.

'When I am with you time stands still. Nothing else is important. I only want you and nothing more.'

We'd only been on a couple of dates, shared a couple of kisses. We were both rowing competitively. I was firefighting and still working two days a week in a physio practice. He ran a cafe in town, so we couldn't see too much of each other. He lived north side, I lived south side, so we made telephone calls and he inundated me with text messages. He had an annoying habit of asking me important things by text. I was in the gym at work one day when he asked if it bothered me that he was a few years younger than me. I thought it an odd question to ask, especially by text. After all, it was only a couple of years. I jokingly replied that surely it would be he who should be worried. Then he asked if we should put our relationship on hold, just be friends until the Australian surf lifesaving titles were over so that I could focus on rowing. No, I answered, confused as to what he was trying to say. He kept telling me how important I was to him, so why did he want to put 'us' on hold?

Men always seemed to fall for me because they saw my strength. When they found the sensitive vulnerable part of me, they didn't want me any more, or at least that's what I believed. 'You don't know me yet,' I warned him. He joked that he'd borrow a sledgehammer to break down my wall. Or did he need something more powerful?

It was about six weeks before we slept together, but we'd still only had a few dates. I was at work the next morning when my phone beeped in my pocket. I pulled it out, opening the message.

'You are the love of my life, the only one I want to be with. I can promise you I will always be here for you. I want to spend my life with you.'

I smiled as I read it, passing blindly over the fact we barely knew each other, for Rob's words gave me everything my heart craved, like feeding heroin to an addict. My wall began to crumble, just as Adam's had.

Why is it, if anyone, or should I say a girl that I begin to like, I grasp on to with my heart ... I am furious with myself for beginning to care in that heart-crippling way of mine for Sarah. The odd thing is, it's just not possible. I have been with the girl for what is it, ten days. What on earth is wrong with me? I am sure it is not that my heart is as sensitive as that.

Rob's words fed fuel to my fairy tale that I could meet a man, fall in love and create the family I never had. As my wall collapsed, so I began to feel vulnerable, reiterating to Rob that he wouldn't love me when he saw the real me. He continued to shower me with reassurance and love, allowing me to trust tentatively in the safety. But surreptitiously his words became doused in his own vulnerability.

'I feel so safe in your arms, a million miles from anything that hurts. You have got inside my heart, so please be gentle with it.'

I kept reassuring him, as he had for me, yet it never seemed to be enough. His messages were laced with need.

'The more I see you and get to know you the more I feel empty when I am alone. I don't need anything else in my world, just you.'

I returned his words; desperate to fill his emptiness. I didn't see the danger. All I saw was that someone needed me. I wasn't helpless. I couldn't rescue Adam but I could rescue Rob. I wanted to reassure him, to reach in and take his pain away. Then I could prove my love, my worthiness. I thought that was what love was. I ignored the annoying sense of unease within me, for I had my fairy tale within reach. I had what I had always thought that I had wanted. I had the fantasy.

Eventually, when I felt safe enough, I told Rob about my family and my fear of loss. I wanted to be honest, to show him who I really was. I let him see my vulnerability. I cried in front of him and he did for me what I had done for him. He took me in his arms, he made me feel safe and he took my pain away.

'Sweetie, nothing will happen to me and I will never leave you. I promise I am here with you and for you, forever.'

Finally I had the feeling that I had craved incessantly ever since my mother's death. I felt warm and safe.

Two days later Rob arrived at my place looking anxious and distant.

'What's up, sweetheart?' I asked.

'I can't do this to you. I don't want to put you through losing anyone again. I think we should break up.'

'What?' I was reeling from the shock. 'I don't understand.' I started to cry. It felt as if I'd taken a king hit from Muhammad Ali. I took slow deep breaths and I squashed the grief down inside me.

'If that is what you want, then there is nothing I can do to stop you,' I said calmly.

He turned his back to leave, hesitating. We both stood separately, oscillating between fear and love, on a ridge, looking left and right.

'Please don't go.'

The words left my mouth involuntarily. He turned toward me from where he stood in the doorway and we reached out for one another, losing ourselves in the safety, in the comfort once more, taking hold of each other's pain and dissolving it. Fear and love sat within the room like twins, confusing us, swapping identities surreptitiously. I no longer knew which was which, for fear engulfs love.

Rob said he'd damaged us with his actions, betrayed my trust. I said he hadn't but my gut told me otherwise.

I think that I may truly believe that a person in essence is his or her instinct. We often curb our instinct and this habit makes us lie …

Emotion clouded my instinct, fear smothered it. In my eyes, to admit the betrayal, to confront him on his about-turn, would have meant to risk the very thing I feared most, to lose someone I loved. So instead I showered Rob with love and reassurance.

One weekend he surprised me with a romantic weekend away in a hotel in the city. We went for dinner at Circular Quay, overlooking the Opera House, and wandered along George Street, holding hands. It was a beautiful evening. I saw a fire truck coming toward us down the street. I raised my arm to wave just as one of the boys leant out of the window, shouting.

'Hey, is that guy Benny still stalking you?'

I laughed, shaking my head as the truck drove off. In an instant the energy between Rob and me changed.

'Who was that?' he asked.

'Just some of the boys from the city I used to work with.'

'Why did they say that? Who's that guy?'

'I don't know. They're just joking. Don't worry about it. I think they're talking about a guy I used to work with.'

'What happened with him?'

'Nothing. I honestly don't even know what they're talking about,' I said with an edge of defensiveness in my voice. 'I've never been out with any of them, never fancied any of them, and nothing has ever happened with any of them.' I added, 'They're probably just trying to wind him up. They do that stuff all the time.'

We went back to the hotel room, but I felt it hanging in the air like the smog Adam talked of in India.

The next day Rob sent me a text when I was at work.

'Please promise me there is nothing going on or has gone on between you and that other guy at work. I can't stop thinking about it'

I was gripped by an unstoppable jealousy that made me unable to be honest with myself. My soul was not mine, but merely a reacting catalyst to another's …

It seemed that, no matter how much I reassured him, it was never enough. Then we started to talk about the last guy I'd been out with. I'd broken up with him four years before but we remained friends.

'Why do you still see him?'

'He's a friend.'

'So you still have feelings for him, then?'

'No.'

'Well then, why are you friends?' Rob's voice changed. It didn't feel loving.

'We just hang out. It's nice to have someone to go to dinner with.'

'So you enjoy spending time with him?'

'Yes, I suppose I do.' It felt like a crime even as I said it.

'So you must still have feelings for him?' Suddenly his tone was cold.

'Well, yes, I still care about him, but I don't love him.' Why did I feel as if I'd done something wrong?

'You just said you didn't have feelings for him.'

I started to get frustrated. I felt like I was being backed into a corner.

'He's a friend. I care about my friends. Nothing has ever happened between us since the day we broke up over four years ago.' And it was the truth.

'So why does he buy you gifts, then?'

'I don't know … because he wants to.'

'He obviously still loves you. You shouldn't have accepted the gifts.'

I looked at Rob. I couldn't understand why it was so important and why I felt I needed to defend myself.

'Maybe I felt guilty that I hurt him.'

'Well, that's not friendship, is it?'

'Um, no, I guess not.' Now I was confused. Maybe I had done something wrong. I could not identify what the emotion was that I felt ricocheting around my body. I was desperate to get out of the coldness for it seemed to slice through the fragile warmth in my heart. I wanted to get away from the ice. Every inch of my body screamed to get out.

I know I should speak out, be open, yet it is in that final moment of imminent confrontation that I am dogged by self-questioning that removes the naturalness of it and so removes its credibility.

Why should I not speak all of my heart to Sarah? Tell what I really have thought. The reason is because I do not love her but her idea, and that in my heart are vain selfish wants that do not coincide with what my sensible mind would prescribe as a suitable mould for my character to be.

'I feel like walking away,' I said quietly in an attempt to change the direction of our circular dance. I didn't know why I said it. I just wanted his love back.

Rob didn't try to stop me and I began to cry. My tears dissolved his anger and with it, his coldness. He comforted me and I basked temporarily in the restoration of warmth and togetherness that I so craved. I persuaded Rob we should see a relationship counsellor. After hearing my family story the counsellor suggested I come on my own. Rob's history wasn't a problem for he had a strong supportive family. I knew I'd had a toughish family life but this was about our relationship, not me. I failed to recall that the therapist I saw with Anthony had said the same thing.

I was due to fly to the UK for a month-long trip that I'd booked before I'd even met Rob. As the time neared, it felt as if he began to withdraw again. He didn't kiss me as much. We didn't sleep together as much. He didn't send me messages every morning any more. They were only little things, or were they? They caused an itch, an inflammation of my old wounds, scratching at my insecurities. The malignant cancer that killed my mother now metastasized once again in my life, subtly yet destructively expressing its symptoms through my conflicted relationship.

'Are you changing your mind about me?' I asked tentatively one evening, seeking reassurance before I left for England.

'I don't know why you even say that,' Rob said. He sounded cold and uninterested. I began to feel nauseous.

Unwittingly, Rob had just thrown petrol on my bonfire. My instinct was right. Now that Rob knew me better he didn't want me any more. Was it instinct or fear masquerading as instinct? My bonfire blazed, sending burning embers flying around my body, lighting spot fires of rejection and loss. What had started as a harmless bonfire without warning became a raging bushfire. Rob didn't give me any water for my fire. He let it burn. I started to cry, once more craving togetherness. Only this time Rob never laid a finger on me. He felt icy cold, merely turning his back on me and rolling away. My throat and chest clamped.

Bushfires create devastation. They destroy homes and lives, leaving a burnt ashen landscape. My fire consumed my body, hijacking my rational thought, my connection to myself. I lay in the dark next to the man I loved, engulfed by a crushing, suffocating aloneness. I could not get clarity, only panic.

The more I sought comfort and compassion the more he turned his back. I was not able to explain my reactions for I did not understand them myself. As with all fires, the smoke obscured my vision. I travelled to the UK hanging by an emotional string, insecurities cascading out of control, feeling him withdraw, slipping out of reach, just like the coffin …

Having left, I am full of this sense of loss. I think of Mum and Dad and all seems so far away, absent and lost …

I didn't receive the texts of undying love I so yearned for. On the phone, Rob felt remote. The more I reached, the further he ran. I had that feeling of living in a bubble again. It felt like it had after Adam died. I felt the familiar lump in my throat, the tightness across my chest. I tried to meditate, I tried to write and I tried to breath. I used every tool I had to try to find some peace, but I could not rid myself of the dread.

Four weeks later, I arrived home. It was a Tuesday evening. I prayed I would melt into Rob's arms at the airport and all my doubt would be gone. I smiled as I saw him. He gave me a hug. I hugged him, clung to him, praying he'd kiss me. He didn't. He felt distant. Why hadn't he kissed me? He said he was exhausted.

'Of course, sweetheart, I understand, go to bed.'

It was 9pm. I tried to hide my disappointment. Once again I lay awake, overcome by a hauntingly familiar yet intangible feeling of fear.

The next morning, Rob left early for work, kissing me briefly on my forehead as he left. I fumbled my way through a day at work, clambering on roofs, repairing storm damage, ensconced in my bubble for my sense of foreboding shadowed me, like a thunderous cloud as I clung to the slates. I could not turn to Rob for help. I could not allow him to see my crumbling self, so I told him I was jet-lagged. I turned instead to one of my closest friends, falling into his warm open arms. I began physically to shake and sob. My body was at the hospital with my aunt once more, twenty-one years later reliving that haunting tidal wave of grief.

After the tidal wave, the desolation set in. I was desperate to reconnect, to pierce my bubble, so I turned to writing. I wrote a long letter to Rob, just as I had for my father. As Adam had said;

I tried to write what I felt, I hope it was okay but then what can be wrong in speaking as you feel, however vulnerable it may leave you ...

I left the letter in his apartment yet he never made any response to it. I went over to his place, hoping to talk. He didn't want to talk. I clawed desperately at the walls of his cave just as I had clawed at my father's tomb of depression. The more I pursued him emotionally the more he distanced me emotionally and physically. He retreated further and further into his cave, reinforcing it with ice. He started avoiding me. I tried to arrange to meet him, yet he'd always find some banal excuse.

Finally, we spoke on the phone and within minutes he blurted out, 'I'm too busy for a girlfriend.'

'What?' I was stunned. 'Are you breaking up with me?'

'I'm just too busy to have a girlfriend.'

And that was it, the end of our short relationship, because he was *'too busy'*.

What about your guarantees and your declarations of everlasting love? You promised you'd never leave me, I pleaded endlessly inside my head.

The last couple of days have been so very thoughtful. I have thought of passion and compassion and why we have curbed it in our words when we feel it so strongly in our hearts.

No answers. No more comfort blanket, just a rejection of my love. It had only been six months yet the intensity of the loss felt like a searing dagger being thrust repeatedly into my chest, shoving me kicking and screaming into the pain. It landed me in a crevasse where the darkness and silence were so familiar to the quicksand after Adam's death that I could not differentiate between the two. I asked myself how such a short relationship could cause me such intense pain. I wondered what was wrong with me.

It felt that if I let go of Rob, I would somehow be letting go of Adam. They were so entangled in my mind and in my heart. *They both left me. Why did they leave me? They said they loved me but they left me anyway. Why did they do that to me? My love wasn't enough. I wasn't enough.* Without their love for me I was nothing.

Then the anger came. I don't like anger. In fact, I hate it. I fear it and avoid it. I wanted to scream at Rob for promising he'd always be there when he wasn't. I wanted to scream at the old lady who had commented on how she didn't care for the likes of Adam in her neighbourhood. I wanted to scream at Adam's ex-girlfriend for hurting him ... at my father for not being there ... at Jo for hurting Adam, and for not being there for us after Mum died. I wanted to lash out and stamp my foot, like a child, for finding myself here, once more, alone.

'It's not fair! Love me, *love* me. If you loved me, you'd be here ...'

Who, who would be here? I hate you all yet I crave your love. My anger mirrored Adam's:

Just the other day I was angry, a nagging frustration making me see the world with spite, hating everything that all these poncey people were fucking about at. The worst of it, there is no vent. I find myself constantly frowning as I wander from here to Hampstead. (God, could be the title of a book ... From here to Hampstead, a pilgrim's guide to puerility.) Unaware of the reason for it. I taunt myself with maybe it's Sarah, but then shrug and say, no the fuck it isn't. I'm just disenchanted, disenchanted with crap.

Months went by and I kept thinking I should be over Rob by now. I started seeing a new therapist, and together we started to dig. Digging was hard. I hit rock after rock, and with every impact I uncovered old injuries. I unearthed skeletons that terrified me, ones I didn't know existed. I didn't know their origins or how deep they were buried.

As we dug, so the panic returned, fear stalking me: my unconscious self in crisis once more. I didn't know that there were predators in crevasses. I thought they were lifeless bar the creaking, groaning, moving ice. But a bird of prey can fly into a crevasse. It can swoop and snarl, sensing vulnerability, smelling blood. It pecked at my chest, leaving me fragile at the bottom of a fathomless crevasse, my heart bleeding, my head bleeding, fragile and motionless.

One night as I lay in bed, in the depths of confused despair, I began to sob uncontrollably, howling. Then, without warning, something intangible swept through my body, and out of that dark moment came a life-changing message of clarity: 'It's just the same old pain, T.' I felt it not just in my head but in the rich red blood that coursed through the capillaries in my heart. That realization felt like a gift for all the pain endured. This was old pain, not new pain. That knowledge sent me on my path to freedom from the past.

CHAPTER 29

I started to gather my tools. Anything I could lay my hands on to help me climb out of the crevasse in which I was trapped. Therapy was my ice axe, helping me to get a foothold to find some steadiness. My friends were my rope, my lifeline. I took pleasure in simple things. I looked after myself in any way I could. I wrote a journal, practised yoga and meditated (if you could call it that). I ate nutritious food, slept well and exercised, all the while storing up energy for the difficult climb ahead.

I turned toward the fear, actively seeking it out so that I could confront it. For me, that meant enrolling in singing lessons. I could run into burning buildings, jump out of planes, smash through waves in a surfboat, but singing terrified me. For as long as I could remember I had mouthed the words to 'Happy Birthday'. I didn't even sing in the shower. I wanted to find my voice, to rid myself of the restriction I felt across my throat. When I stood in front of the mirror with my aptly named singing teacher Joy looking on I saw my vulnerability staring back at me. I saw my inner child hiding behind the chair in our living room and I wanted to cry. When I finally made a sound, standing in front of that mirror, it was as if vomit was rising from within, an overwhelming rush of emotion coursing through my body as if I was vomiting up the self-hatred.

Joy told me that singing was about allowing oneself to be vulnerable. Perhaps it was for that reason that I dreaded every single lesson I attended, but I left every one, without fail, feeling empowered. Needless to say, the boys at work, being eager as ever to help, proceeded to burst into song every time they saw me, even singing rather than speaking the odd radio message. I remain a terrible singer, but I faced the fear and found my voice and I no longer mouth the words to 'Happy Birthday'.

When I opened my heart to Rob I found a frightened teenage girl huddled alone in the corner of a dark room. It was time to step into that room as the strong, grounded, mature adult Tara. Rob's desertion forced me to revisit my past; that was his gift to me. I had thought he had come into my life to be my lover, my husband, the father of my children. I had so desperately wanted that. As it turned out, Rob allowed me to access a layer of grief that up until this time had entombed my heart. It had prevented me from living my life fully, and it was not allowing me to love.

Sue, my therapist, said I had 'faulty thinking' with regard to love and anger.

'Great,' I thought. 'I have faulty thinking.'

Slowly we began to unravel my carefully sculpted but apparently 'warped' patterns of thinking.

My shunning of anger spoke volumes about my need for approval, for support, for validation and most of all for love. My heart saw Adam's suicide as the ultimate rejection of me and my love. For me, anger and love could not co-exist, so when the anger came, I syphoned it off to those around me, to anyone, just so long as it wasn't directed toward Adam.

I loved Adam so dearly, so avidly and idealistically, that I could not contaminate that love with any negative emotion. I stole my idea of love from the memory of a nineteen-year-old idealist and romantic and I carried that ideal with me for over twenty years.

*I suppose at heart I am an idealist and, however much I can see
that maybe idealism is the punch-bag of realism for me, it holds a
greater truth. For, is not an ideal a perfection?*

No one ever lived up to Adam, the purity of love I held for
him. I was safe and Adam was safe so long as nothing challenged
my fairy tale of Adam and me. The irony was, this very fairy tale
denied me a chance at love. I did not want to admit that it had
been Adam who had asked the ultimate forgiveness of me, and
that it was he who had let me down, who had left me alone with
my pain. I closed my eyes and pictured my brother and me …

I am standing on the side of my mountain. I have stopped
walking, stopped my heavy trudge. I notice the weight upon me
and the darkness of my cloak. I stand in the silence of nature
with the soft wind upon my face. I speak with my brother.
  'Did I let you down, Ad? Did I?'
  In the silence, he speaks to me softly and with tenderness.
'No, you didn't let me down – I let you down.'
  I look at him and he at me and for the first time I acknowledge
softly, 'Yes, you did.' We are standing, looking at each other,
two souls touching each other in the field of nature.
  'What should I do, dear brother? Please tell me. Help me.'
  'Go forward without me, my beautiful sister. Let me go. Let
me lie here. You don't need me any more. Go live your life as
you want it to be, embrace it, have passion, be free of me.'
  I stand still, looking at my brother, my other half, my mirrored
soul, my heart – yet also my burden, my chains, my cloak. I look
up ahead of me uncertainly, oscillating between the past and
the future, the solitude and uncertainty of the way up versus
the familiarity and comfort of the path behind me. Adam nods
at me reassuringly. He lifts his hand to take my cloak. I remain
still, torn. The wind stops. My brother nods once more in an
unspoken gift of freedom.
  I begin to walk tentatively, checking to look back all the
while, still seeing my brother looking at me – nodding, smiling

his beautiful radiant smile. I keep walking, my feet feeling firmer on the ground, looking back less often until I turn and Adam is just a spot on the horizon. I cannot let him go completely. I need to be able to see him, to be able to check he is okay. Just the line of sight, that's all, enough to keep the cord alive.

I realize now that Adam grew with me over all these years. I held on to him so tightly, preserving him avidly in my heart. I built a story in my head of Adam my perfect brother. I placed him carefully upon a pedestal where I could protect and love him. I would carry him with me always and I would live for him. I would live his hopes for himself and for me. The story I built helped me cope.

What would Adam's hopes for me have been? He would have wanted me to be happy. He would have wanted me to go on with my life and move on from his death, to live a full, happy, adventurous life. It would have devastated him to think of me still living in pain from his death, still idolizing him.

Little by little, I find that my actions seem no longer to be driven by fear but rather by a desire for wholeness, for trust in myself and the world about me, and freedom from the past. I find that I am much better these days at sitting outside myself and observing my actions, my thoughts, my feelings. I have learned to sit in the pain when it's there, to observe it, identify it and acknowledge it, to respect it and let it be, until such time that it passes, just as a cloud passes across a mountain. It may hover for a while or it may pass swiftly through, for pain, like happiness and peace, is transient. Just as Adam said:

Everything finds its place, just as the colour and the beauty do, so does the pain.

I trust myself more and I forgive myself a little better for not being perfect, for not always being true to myself. I'm not perfect and my brother wasn't perfect and that's okay. It doesn't mean I love him any the less or love myself any less. It just means I'm human; I'm still learning and I'm doing the best that I can. I stopped torturing myself in the way my brother had when he wrote: *I have cried all my life because I wasn't perfect and I couldn't accept it …*

Maybe, just maybe, I am worthy of love with all my imperfections. I'm learning lessons that might allow me to make a difference to the lives of others. That's all I could wish or hope for, for myself and for my brother, to know that, between us, we made a difference. Now, when I look into my heart I see a young woman standing openly in the middle of the room, half in darkness, half in light, turning calmly toward the sun.

I used to think that when I achieved some milestone or some confrontation of fear, like going to India, writing letters to my mum and brother, going back to Oxford, having therapy or writing this book, that the grief would end, I'd be done. As if I could put a full stop on that part of my life so that I could begin the next. There is no end to grief: it is not linear, there is no finish line, no destination to be reached. There is no time frame. We navigate it, as we navigate our lives: some people come our way, some stay, others leave; jobs change, home changes, goals change.

And, while I believe there is no end to grief, the same is true of healing, and with healing comes hope, self-discovery and clarity. Now, whenever a wave of grief sweeps over me, I look on it as an opportunity, a chance to peel back another layer so I may get closer to my true self, to what lies within, for the deeper the grief, the greater the opportunity for learning. The time had finally come to let Adam go, to hold the love but shed the burden, as Adam had done when he had chosen to end his life.

Dear Adam,
My gorgeous brother – I keep thinking of your words … 'All my hopes lie with Tara.'
I have been living by those words for so many years. I took the cup you offered me with open arms. It was a cup bursting and

overflowing with the nectar of other people's expectations. The cup gave me hope and purpose – a reason to live at a time when I could find no reason within myself. When I took that cup it meant I could live with you still in my heart, live your life for you, for to imagine that loss to myself and the world was simply too much to bear. I could make you proud and be the person you wanted to be as well as the person you wanted me to be.

Slowly, Ad, ever so slowly I realize I am me and you are you. I am different to you. I have my own values, my own hopes, my own decisions, my own failings, my own misgivings and my own experiences – I have my own path.

For so many years we have travelled that path together. I have carried you with me always – protecting you, loving you, defending you, cherishing you, trying so desperately to give you the life you couldn't have – the life that you gave away. That was the dream that I had of you and me, so many years ago in India on that dusty path – you leaning on me, me buckling under the weight yet still clinging to you, the scream for help that would not come, the stifling suffocating weight of our aloneness.

I feel it's time now for me to ever so gently let you down off my shoulders to let you stand alone as you – as Adam the smart, beautiful, caring, compassionate soulful nineteen-year-old.

It's time for me to walk alone now, to carry less weight upon my shoulders, be free to breathe life and fresh air into my soul – to feel it run through me and walk my own path.

Perhaps we can walk side by side on our parallel paths – each on our own mountain range, glancing at each other, waving, smiling, singing, dancing. I could blow you a kiss across the valley; it would meander softly in the wind toward you where it could come to settle gently on your cheek, carrying with it all the purity and tenderness of the love of a sister for her brother.

Would that be okay, my gorgeous brother? Can we do that for each other? Can you help me shed the chains and cords of constant restraint so that I may embrace my freedom and my life with open arms and a lightness of being – so that I can be me?

I love you, Adam. Let's set that poisoned cup aside, let's leave it behind, locked safely away beneath the ground where it can be of no harm to another soul. Then let's start walking separately as our paths diverge, waving at each other, enjoying the beauty of our own journey, our own mountain range, our own paths. Yours may be shorter than mine, but it stands alone in its uniqueness. Your footprints remain and there are many for whom those footprints shed light and gave direction to their own path. Rest peacefully, dear brother, at the end of your path. I will be looking, glancing back at you from time to time, always admiring you, always loving you, always appreciating what I learned from you. May we both love and cherish our freedom, our uniqueness while always holding our love for each other and for life.

Be free …

Peace comes in inches – it comes in degrees and it comes in percentages, just like healing …

I no longer see what life took from me – I see what it gave me.

EPILOGUE

Woollahra Fire Station, Sydney, 2012

It's Friday night and I'm in the mess room at the fire station. I've just cooked myself a beautiful salmon fillet. Yes, salmon again, although not fishcakes this time and I've only cooked for myself. The selfometer is creeping up.

I'm just tucking into my first mouthful as the bells go.

'Bugger,' I mutter under my breath.

I'm on the ladders tonight, though. The boys have been kind to me as it's an extra shift I'm doing for someone else. The ladder truck doesn't turn out to every job so it's quieter than being on the pump. The bells are getting louder. I wait for the voice.

'Automatic fire alarm, Ladders 11.' I'm surprised: the ladders don't usually turn out to automatic fire alarms.

I stand up, swallowing my mouthful of food, looking wistfully at the perfect medium rare salmon fillet sitting on my plate.

'That's us,' I hear Digby, also known as 'Big Dog', call out. He's driving the ladders tonight. I'm the 'offsider', which means that if we get a job I'm in the basket at the top of the ladder.

'It's at the Maroubra Seals Club', Digby shouts.

I'm grabbing my turn-out pants and jacket, zipping up my boots. Lights and sirens on, we pull out of the station. We hear the radio call.

'Red Red Red ... Third Alarm ...'

'It's going,' says Digby calmly.

197

A red message means it's a priority. All other messages stop. Second alarm means they need more trucks. It's a big job. Digby puts his foot down a little harder on the accelerator.

I wriggle into my safety harness, not an easy feat when you're flying around corners at a rapid rate of knots. To this day Digby looks at me when we talk about it and shakes his head.

'How the hell did you do that?'

'Yoga,' I smile and wink at him.

Even from a few kilometres away we see the plumes of smoke and flame billowing into the night sky. We pull up on the corner of the building, fire trucks appearing from every direction. We are the first aerial appliance there. The fire's on the roof of the building, a large multi-purpose club on the beach front. We start to set the truck up. They are having difficulty accessing the fire from inside the building.

Digby and I work together. We know our roles. I run the hose up the ladder bank, get the monitor set up, grab my breathing apparatus and hook up my harness to the cage. Digby runs the hose from the hydrant, through the pump and into the ladders truck. I slip the hand-held radio transmitter into the pocket of my jacket.

I turn to Digby and give the signal, pushing my foot on the rather unfortunately named 'dead man's' pedal. I hear the engine rev and use the levers to elevate the ladder cage. I'm moving up, higher into the sky. I'm listening to the radio messages.

'Intense heat, risk of roof collapse.'

I know they need water from above. I can see the fire clearly now, in the back corner of the building. If I put water on to it while firefighters are inside I could kill them as the weight of the water can cause an already-fragile roof to cave in.

I look down at the ground beneath me. I see reams of hose, like a plate of spaghetti. Firefighters working away like ants. I'm waiting for water.

❋

Finally, through the Darth Vader-like sound of my own breath in my mask, I hear the call.

'All firefighters clear. Get the aerial to work.'

'Water on,' comes the voice across the radio.

'Water on,' I confirm as I manoeuvre the cage of the ladder truck into position, feeling the water pressure build like a worm burrowing through its cave.

Eventually the water blasts from the monitor, sending a jet stream out toward the burning building. I'm perched high in the sky, alone at the top of the ladder. The wind is gusty, enveloping me in smoke when it swirls unexpectedly. I'm breathing compressed air through the breathing apparatus on my back. The flames rage angrily, throwing embers into the night sky. I blast the jet of water, changing the spray, adjusting for the wind. Slowly the flames subside, almost whimpering as they succumb to the incessant torrent of water. Calm prevails. The smoke clears.

Afterword

'That which does not kill us makes us stronger'
Friedrich Nietzsche

Looking at Tara's powerful memoir from the perspective of a positive psychologist, I see that she offers a message of hope for those of us who have suffered the premature loss of loved ones. Her story demonstrates that it is possible not only to survive tragedy but also, ultimately, to grow from it. When she says, *'I no longer see what life took from me – I see what it gave me,'* what she is describing is post-traumatic growth (PTG), the positive psychological changes that can occur after a life-changing trauma shatters our assumptions about life. People who have experienced PTG have been found to have a changed sense of priorities, a greater appreciation of life, stronger connections to others and a richer spiritual life; they have a better sense of their talents and abilities and see new possibilities and pathways for their life. What helps people toward PTG rather than post-traumatic stress disorder (PTSD) is finding a way of accommodating the tragedy into their mental landscape. Life won't ever be the same but eventually they can pick up the pieces and put life back together in a fresh, different form that holds appeal for them.

Tara's story reveals many of the routes to resilience, another key term in positive psychology, which helps us cope and move forward after suffering a tragedy. To borrow a metaphor from Tara's love of rowing, your resilience is like the sea level. Imagine you're in a boat. When life is difficult and your resilience is low you are more likely to crash into the rocks. But when you feed your wellbeing by engaging in activities that help you feel good and function well, the water level rises to the point where you are able to sail over those rocks. This book contains evidence-based paths to resilience, starting with the act of writing itself.

Tara writes letters to her family, both dead and alive, to process her grief. This is expressive writing. Writing or talking about traumatic experiences can help make sense of what has happened and transform, solidify or highlight important aspects of life. Although the process itself may feel upsetting, even a few short writing sessions have been shown to have psychological benefits and such activity can also have value for physical health, revealed in better immune system functioning and fewer physical illnesses further down the line.

Having a sense of meaning and purpose is also a significant ingredient in recovering wellbeing. Tara's desire to fulfil her mother's wish for her to lead a useful life is an example of that. A purpose in life gives us a solid bedrock of meaning which can help us be resilient, as well as being a target to aim for. Investing effort into something meaningful can grant us a sense of fulfilment and satisfaction in life. In fact, we are more likely to construct a life purpose from *negative* events, asking ourselves, 'What does this mean for my life and how can I make something of it?' Going beyond the self in the service of something meaningful is a source of 'eudaimonic wellbeing' – a deeper dimension of happiness.

Another fundamental need is relatedness – having a sense of connection and belonging. Positive psychologist Chris Peterson once said that we could sum up the science of happiness in three words: *other people matter.* We need other people for our wellbeing. Reaching out to people builds resilience and often involves someone outside the immediate family, as in Tara's case with her Aunt Margaret. Tara also reaches out through therapy, and goes on to create a caring social circle with other firefighters in Australia.

If the body is well fed, exercised and slept, it can be a powerful instrument to support resilience. Physical activity can provide emotional first-aid to help us move through waves of intense emotions. Tara describes her joy at hiking in the mountains and rowing on the ocean. It only takes around 10 minutes of this 'green exercise' – physical activity in a natural environment – to produce positive emotions.

Creative activities, as well as physical pursuits, are routes into flow, the state of being 'in the zone' in which we are so absorbed in what we're doing that we lose track of time. If we are depressed and positive emotions seem like too much of a stretch, flow can be easier to access. Following our passions is the easiest way of finding flow.

Our passions are clues to where our strengths lie. We may lose sight of these when we're low or vulnerable, and fixate on our weaknesses. Engaging our strengths will strengthen our resilience. They are inner resources that help us resolve problems and move through periods of difficulty. The strength of optimism, for instance, protects against depression. Courage, kindness, future-mindedness and perseverance are other strengths that protect us from mental illness. Studies have shown that finding new ways of using our strengths builds wellbeing and reduces the symptoms of depression. Tara engages her strengths by going back to sport and we see her going from strength to strength.

Tara writes, *'One of the endlessly beautiful things about life is that it is constantly changing.'* Humans are hardy creatures. People do come through traumatic experiences and go on to live good lives and even find positives in the most negative of events. Optimism can be hard to muster on the journey to recovery. Hope, on the other hand, is a practical concept in positive psychology. It is made up of two components – motivation or agency (willpower) and finding pathways to the goal (waypower). Or to put it another way: where there is a will to transcend tragedy there is almost certainly a way.

Miriam Akhtar
www.positivepsychologytraining.co.uk
@pospsychologist

DOS AND DON'TS OF TALKING TO SOMEONE IF YOU ARE CONCERNED THEY MAY BE HAVING THOUGHTS OF SUICIDE

Do...

- Ask the person how they are feeling.
- Listen non-judgmentally and be supportive.
- Mention 'the word' and ask the question, 'Are you having thoughts of suicide?'
- Let the person know that you care and you want to help.
- Get informed yourself and seek help from any of the resources listed on pages 206–9.
- *Be there* even if you don't know what to say. Just listen.
- Encourage the person to seek help and explore all options.
- Ask the person how you can help them.
- Help that person to *stay safe* by removing things that could be used for self-harm and ensuring they have someone with them at all times.

- Help the person to write a list of the positive things in their life and the people that care.
- Look out for warning signs, such as marked changes in behaviour or the person saying things like 'You'd be better off without me.'
- Find out what support is available.
- Offer to accompany the person to appointments if they agree.
- Create a support plan with the person, including contact details of close friends and family, mental health helplines and 24-hour services available.
- Let the person know that thoughts of suicide are often associated with a treatable mental illness and that suicide is a permanent solution to a temporary problem.
- Undertake a recognized suicide-prevention training course such as ASIST, run through Living Works (see page 208).

Don't...

- Judge. No one can be wrong about how they feel.
- Avoid the topic of suicide.
- Express shock at what the person tells you.
- Tell someone what is best for them.
- Lecture the person on the value of life.
- Try to use guilt or threats to prevent suicide.
- Be sworn to secrecy. Instead, try to gain informed consent from the person to seek support.

RESOURCES

I hope you find the following list of resources useful. Of course it's by no means exhaustive, but it's based on those services that I feel provide accessible, relevant, up-to-date and evidence-based information and support for anyone affected by mental illness, grief or suicide.

Some Specific Suicide-prevention Resources

International Association for Suicide Prevention: www.iasp.info
A global information manual with a comprehensive resource section, including contacts and crisis information.

Papyrus: www.papyrus-uk.org
A UK organization dedicated to helping prevent youth suicide and giving young people hope.

American Foundation for Suicide Prevention: www.afsp.org
Aims to help people understand and prevent suicide through research and education.

Immediate Help in a Crisis
Phonelines available 24 hours a day, seven days a week:

Befrienders Worldwise: www.befrienders.org
Provides emotional support to prevent suicide and local helplines around the world.

Australia: Lifeline Australia: 13 11 14

UK: Samaritans: 08457 90 90 90

USA: National Suicide Prevention Lifeline: 1 800 273 8255

Mental Health Organizations

Australia:
The Black Dog Institute: www.blackdoginstitute.org.au
Offers comprehensive information and resources for all mood disorders
with a great library of fact sheets and self-test questionnaires.

SANE Australia: www.sane.org
Provides resources (including fact sheets and podcasts), training,
support and advice for anyone who is affected by mental illness.

UK:
Mind: www.mind.org.uk
A comprehensive mental-health website that provides advice,
information and support to anyone experiencing a mental illness,
as well as campaigning to raise awareness and understanding and
improve services.

SANE: www.sane.org.uk
Provides help and support for anyone experiencing a mental illness
as well as raising awareness and understanding of mental illness in
the community.

Young Minds: www.youngminds.org.uk
Information about child and adolescent mental health. Services for
parents and professionals.

USA:
National Institute of Mental Health: www.nimh.nih.gov
US government website with excellent, up-to-date information about
mental illness and suicide, with access to downloadable booklets and
fact sheets.

US government mental health site: www.mentalhealth.gov
Aims to educate the public and professionals on all issues relating to
mental health. Also provides information about where to get help.

Grief and Bereavement

Australia:
The National Centre for Childhood Grief: www.childhoodgrief.org.au
Provides support for bereaved children in Australia.

Australian Centre for Grief and Bereavement: www.grief.org.au
Provides support for bereaved people through research, education and consultancy.

UK:
Cruse Bereavement Care: www.cruse.org.uk
Offers face-to-face, telephone, email and website support.

Survivors of Bereavement by Suicide: www.uk-sobs.org.uk
Offers support and information for those bereaved by suicide.

Winston's Wish: www.winstonswish.org.uk
Provides support specifically for bereaved children in the UK.

USA:
National Alliance for Grieving Children: www.childrengrieve.org
Advice, support and information for bereaved children.

The Center for Complicated Grief: www.complicatedgrief.org
Help and support for those suffering from complicated grief.

Training Courses for People Supporting Those with Mental Illness

Mental Health First Aid:
www.mhfa.com.au/cms/international-mhfa-programs
Australia: **www.mhfa.com.au**
UK: **www.mhfaengland.org**
USA: **www.mentalhealthfirstaid.org**
Mental Health First Aid provides training packages all over the world that teach how to help people who may be developing a mental illness or who are in crisis.

Living Works: www.livingworks.net
International suicide-intervention training.

Online Free E-learning Sites for Depression and Anxiety:

Mood gym: www.moodgym.anu.edu.au
Cognitive behaviour therapy skills for treating depression.

e-couch: www.ecouch.anu.edu.au
Modules on depression, anxiety, loss and grief.

My Compass: www.mycompass.org.au
Self-help service aiming to promote resilience and wellbeing.

Books

Personal Growth and Development
Frankl, Viktor E, *Man's Search for Meaning*, Rider & Co, 2011
Peck, Scott M, *The Road Less Travelled*, Touchstone Books, 1997

Depression
Akhtar, Miriam, *Positive Psychology for Overcoming Depression,* Watkins
    Publishing, 2012
Gilbert, Paul, *Overcoming Depression*, Robinson Publishing, 2009
Williams, Mark, John Teasdale, Zindel Segal and Jon Kabat-Zin,
    The Mindful Way Through Depression, Guildford Press, 2007

Anxiety and Stress
Lejeune, Chad, *The Worry Trap*, New Harbinger Publications, 2007
Follette, Victoria and Jacqueline Pistorello, *Finding Life Beyond Trauma*,
    New Harbinger Publications, 2007
Marks, Isaac, *Living with Fear*, McGraw-Hill, 2005

Suicide
Ellis, Thomas E, *Choosing to Live*, New Harbinger Publications, 1996
    (Self-help for those who are considering suicide.)

Grief
Albom, Mitch, *The Five People You Meet in Heaven*, Little, Brown, 2003
Lewis, C S, *A Grief Observed*, Faber & Faber, 1961
McKissock, Mal, *Coping with Grief*, fourth edition, Kindle, 2012

Mum and Dad's wedding, 6 August 1966. This is the hat
Dad wore to the beach on honeymoon ... as you do!

The three Lal musketeers in happy times on holiday in 1979, just before
we buried Adam in that hole in the sand!

Mum and me in 1984. A treasured moment of affection on what would end up being our last family holiday. It was this haven of maternal warmth and love that I would spend my life searching to recreate.

Adam and me, Christmas 1987. Another of Adam's and my party tricks, once we progressed from standing on each other's shoulders.

WATKINS

Sharing Wisdom Since
1893

The story of Watkins Publishing dates back to March 1893, when John M. Watkins, a scholar of esotericism, overheard his friend and teacher Madame Blavatsky lamenting the fact that there was nowhere in London to buy books on mysticism, occultism or metaphysics. At that moment Watkins was born, soon to become the home of many of the leading lights of spiritual literature, including Carl Jung, Rudolf Steiner, Alice Bailey and Chögyam Trungpa.

Today our passion for vigorous questioning is still resolute. With over 350 titles on our list, Watkins Publishing reflects the development of spiritual thinking and new science over the past 120 years. We remain at the cutting edge, committed to publishing books that change lives.

DISCOVER MORE ...

Read our blog

Watch and listen to
our authors in action

Sign up to
our mailing list

JOIN IN THE CONVERSATION

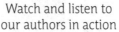

WatkinsPublishing   @watkinswisdom

WatkinsPublishingLtd   +watkinspublishing1893

Our books celebrate conscious, passionate, wise and happy living.
Be part of the community by visiting

www.watkinspublishing.com